Budget
of the
US Government
Fiscal Year 2022

Budget of the United States Government, Fiscal Year 2022 contains the Budget Message of the President, information on the President's priori ties, and summary tables.

This information is useful for businesses, local governments, associations, scholars, and students who wish to study the budget in a written format.

Should you have suggestions or feedback on ways to improve this book please send email to Books@OcotilloPress.com

Edited 2021 Ocotillo Press
ISBN 978-1-954285-66-8

Ocotillo Press
Houston, TX 77017
Books@OcotilloPress.com

Disclaimer: The user of this book is responsible for following safe and lawful practices at all times. The publisher assumes no responsibility for the use of the content of this book. The publisher has made an effort to ensure that the text is complete and properly typeset, however omissions, errors, and other issues may exist that the publisher is unaware of.

BUDGET
OF THE U.S.
GOVERNMENT

FISCAL YEAR 2022

OFFICE OF MANAGEMENT AND BUDGET

THE WHITE HOUSE
WASHINGTON

THE BUDGET DOCUMENTS

Budget of the United States Government, Fiscal Year 2022 contains the Budget Message of the President, information on the President's priorities, and summary tables.

Analytical Perspectives, Budget of the United States Government, Fiscal Year 2022 contains analyses that are designed to highlight specified subject areas or provide other significant presentations of budget data that place the budget in perspective. This volume includes economic and accounting analyses, information on Federal receipts and collections, analyses of Federal spending, information on Federal borrowing and debt, baseline or current services estimates, and other technical presentations.

Supplemental tables and other materials that are part of the *Analytical Perspectives* volume are available at https://whitehouse.gov/omb/analytical-perspectives/.

Appendix, Budget of the United States Government, Fiscal Year 2022 contains detailed information on the various appropriations and funds that constitute the budget and is designed primarily for the use of the Appropriations Committees. The *Appendix* contains more detailed financial information on individual programs and appropriation accounts than any of the other budget documents. It includes for each agency: the proposed text of appropriations language; budget schedules for each account; legislative proposals; narrative explanations of each budget account; and proposed general provisions applicable to the appropriations of entire agencies or group of agencies. Information is also provided on certain activities whose transactions are not part of the budget totals.

BUDGET INFORMATION AVAILABLE ONLINE

The President's Budget and supporting materials are available online at https://whitehouse.gov/omb/budget/. This link includes electronic versions of all the budget volumes, supplemental materials that are part of the *Analytical Perspectives* volume, spreadsheets of many of the budget tables, and a public use budget database. This link also includes *Historical Tables* that provide data on budget receipts, outlays, surpluses or deficits, Federal debt, and Federal employment over an extended time period, generally from 1940 or earlier to 2022 or 2026. Also available are links to documents and materials from budgets of prior years.

For more information on access to electronic versions of the budget documents, call (202) 512-1530 in the D.C. area or toll-free (888) 293-6498. To purchase the printed documents call (202) 512-1800.

GENERAL NOTES

1. All years referenced for budget data are fiscal years unless otherwise noted. All years referenced for economic data are calendar years unless otherwise noted.
2. Detail in this document may not add to the totals due to rounding.

U.S. GOVERNMENT PUBLISHING OFFICE, WASHINGTON 2021

Table of Contents

THE BUDGET MESSAGE OF THE PRESIDENT

To the Congress of the United States:

Where we choose to invest speaks to what we value as a Nation.

This year's Budget, the first of my Presidency, is a statement of values that define our Nation at its best. It is a Budget for what our economy can be, who our economy can serve, and how we can build it back better by putting the needs, goals, ingenuity, and strength of the American people front and center.

The Budget is built around a fundamental understanding of how our economy works and why, for too long and for too many, it has not. It is a Budget that reflects the fact that trickle-down economics has never worked, and that the best way to grow our economy is not from the top down, but from the bottom up and the middle out. Our prosperity comes from the people who get up every day, work hard, raise their family, pay their taxes, serve their Nation, and volunteer in their communities. If we make that understanding our foundation, everything we build upon it will be strong.

And we have already seen how that economic vision is working. When I took office, America was a Nation in crisis. A once-in-a-century pandemic was raging, claiming thousands of American lives each day. A punishing economic crisis had erased 22 million jobs in just 2 months in the spring of 2020 and upended the lives of millions more. The pain these crises caused was visible not just in the data, but in the lives of millions of Americans: Americans who faced an empty chair at the dinner table where a loved one once sat; who had to shut down the family business; who lined up for miles in their cars waiting for a box of food to be put in the trunk; who went to bed staring at the ceiling wondering how they would get through tomorrow.

Through the American Rescue Plan, we answered the emergency and provided desperately needed relief to hundreds of millions of Americans. Immediately, the law began delivering shots in arms and checks in pockets.

The American Rescue Plan is also helping schools reopen safely, helping child care centers stay in business, and helping families pay for child care. In fact, it is providing the largest investment in American child care since World War II. It is delivering food and nutrition assistance to millions of Americans facing hunger. It is providing rental assistance to keep people from being evicted from their homes. It is helping small businesses and restaurants stay open or re-open. It is making healthcare more affordable. It is supporting the recovery of State and local governments. And it is putting us on track to cut child poverty in half this year.

With the resources provided by the American Rescue Plan, we are turning the corner on the pandemic, and powering an equitable economic recovery. In my first 100 days in office, our economy created more than 1.5 million jobs, the most in the first 100 days of any President on record. But more work remains—not simply to emerge from the immediate crises we inherited, but to build back better.

The Budget lays out the essential investments that my Administration has proposed through the American Jobs Plan and the American Families Plan.

The American Jobs Plan puts millions of Americans to work to build our Nation back not just to the way it was before the pandemic, but back better. Americans will rebuild America's transportation infrastructure, water infrastructure, and broadband connectivity infrastructure. Americans will build a clean energy future while investing in communities at risk of being left behind during our energy transition. American workers and American farmers will make unprecedented progress in our effort to tackle climate change. And, thanks to the biggest increase in non-defense research and development spending on record, Americans will boost America's innovative edge in markets where global leadership is up for grabs—markets like battery technology, biotechnology, computer chips, and clean energy. Finally, the American Jobs Plan will create new and better jobs for caregiving workers who have been underpaid and undervalued for far too long.

The American Families Plan addresses four of the biggest challenges facing American families today, and lays the groundwork for individual, family, community, and national success tomorrow. It guarantees four additional years of education for every American, beginning with 2 years of universal high-quality pre-school for every 3- and 4-year old in America, and adding 2 years of free community college. It would make college more affordable and tackle equity gaps with increased Pell grants and investments in institutions serving low-income, first generation students, and students of color. And it provides access to quality, affordable child care to low- and middle-income families, expanded access to healthy meals because no child in America should be hungry or under-nourished, comprehensive paid family and medical leave, and expanded game-changing tax credits for families and workers.

The Budget complements these historic plans with additional proposals to reinvest in the foundations of our Nation's strength—expanding economic opportunity, improving education, tackling the climate crisis, and ensuring a strong national defense while restoring America's place in the world. In the 1950s, our Department of Defense created a Defense Advanced Research Projects Agency (DARPA) to enhance our national security, and DARPA's work helped lead to the creation of the internet, Global Positioning System, and more. The Budget would create an Advanced Research Projects Agency for Health tasked with developing a new generation of medical breakthroughs—marshalling our Nation's incredible scientific capacity to help prevent, detect, and treat diseases like cancer, diabetes, and Alzheimer's. And it calls on the Congress to make progress on healthcare by cutting prescription drug costs and expanding and improving the Affordable Care Act, Medicaid, and Medicare coverage.

The Budget invests directly in the American people and will strengthen our Nation's economy and improve our long-run fiscal health. It reforms our broken tax code to reward work instead of wealth, while also fully paying for the American Jobs Plan and the American Families Plan over 15 years. It will help us build a recovery that is broad-based, inclusive, sustained, and strong. And it will demonstrate to the American people that we value them and that we recognize that they are the key to our shared prosperity; that their Government sees them, hears them, and is able to deliver for them again.

It will send to the world the message that I shared with a Joint Session of the Congress in April: that America is on the move again, and that our democracy is proving it can deliver for our people and is poised to win the competition for the 21st Century.

There are many challenges ahead. But every time America has faced moments of testing, we have emerged stronger. And I believe this Budget will help us become stronger than ever.

I look forward to working with the Congress to deliver on this agenda this year.

JOSEPH R. BIDEN, JR.

THE WHITE HOUSE.

CONFRONTING THE PANDEMIC AND RESCUING THE ECONOMY

America has always been defined by the grit and determination of its people, and our capacity to come together in common purpose at moments of great challenge. Across the generations, that spirit of resilience has seen us through war and depression, natural disasters and disease, and countless crises that have tested the Nation's strength, persistence, and commitment to core values and to one another. For more than a year, we have confronted a confluence of challenges that have called on that resilience like never before.

Inheriting Historic Challenges

When the President took office, America was in the grips of the worst pandemic in a century and a painful economic downturn that had up-ended virtually every aspect of American life. By January, more than 24 million Americans across the Nation had contracted COVID-19. Infection rates and hospitalizations were soaring. More than 400,000 Americans had lost their lives and thousands were dying every single day. A more contagious variant of the virus had begun appearing in communities across America.

Meanwhile, the Administration inherited a disorganized and ineffective national vaccination effort that was struggling to get off the ground. When the President took office, only eight percent of America's seniors—and very few working-age adults—had received their first shot. At the same time, more than 10 months into the COVID-19 pandemic, the Nation still lacked adequate testing capacity and faced shortages of supplies like basic protective equipment for those working on the frontlines.

The broad failure to control the spread of COVID-19 in the months before the President took office had devastating and far-reaching consequences. Millions of students and parents were forced to navigate the challenges of remote learning—straining countless families and disproportionately affecting Black, Hispanic, Asian, and Native American students, as well as students with disabilities and English language learners. Disruptive changes in people's daily lives also took a significant toll on both mental and physical health. Medically fragile individuals and those with chronic diseases such as hypertension, obesity, and diabetes had to make the decision to either protect their health and avoid a negative outcome from COVID-19, or risk losing their jobs. More Americans reported experiencing symptoms of anxiety, overdose deaths rose, and domestic violence surged. Moreover, the COVID-19 pandemic exposed and exacerbated deeply rooted health inequities in the Nation and laid bare gaps and weaknesses in America's public health infrastructure.

As the virus tore across America, it left enormous economic damage in its wake. In January, more than 10 million Americans were out of work, with a national unemployment rate of 6.3 percent. After accounting for workers who either dropped out of the labor force or could not find full-time work, the unemployment rate was over 12 percent. More than 52 percent of America's unemployed had been jobless for more than 15 weeks, a level of long-term unemployment unseen since the depths of the Great Recession. In addition, 1 in 11 Black workers and 1 in 12 Latino workers were unemployed.

Thousands of small businesses closed their doors—many permanently—with many others struggling to stay afloat.

The jobs crisis was particularly severe among women. When the President took office, a staggering 2.5 million women had dropped out of the labor force due to the COVID-19 pandemic—many to help care for their children, with potential lifetime consequences in terms of economic security. Between February 2020 and January 2021, the labor force participation rate for women dropped by 3.7 percent overall, 6.4 percent for Black women, and 6.6 percent for Hispanic women, eviscerating more than 35 years of progress in labor force participation in just one year. The economy was hit hardest in female dominated industries like retail and restaurants. On top of the job loss in those sectors, women working on the frontlines of the COVID-19 pandemic in nursing homes and hospitals—many of whom are often low-paid women of color—risked their health and scrambled to take care of their own families so they could care for others. Early childhood and child care providers—a significant share of which are owned by women and people of color—have also been devastated by the COVID-19 pandemic. Estimates suggest that among child care providers open at the beginning of the COVID-19 pandemic, as of December 2020, roughly one in four were closed.

As a result of this enormous economic disruption, countless Americans who were financially stretched even before the COVID-19 pandemic were plunged into an economic emergency. One in three households struggled to afford basic expenses. Millions of households reported not having enough to eat. Millions of Americans fell behind on their rent or mortgage payments, with more than 15 million households reporting overdue payments when the President took office. Roughly two to three million people lost employer sponsored health insurance between March and September. Further, going into the COVID-19 pandemic, about 30 million people lacked coverage, limiting their access to the healthcare system when the COVID-19 pandemic struck.

Delivering Immediate Relief: Passing the American Rescue Plan Act of 2021

In the face of these twin public health and economic crises, the President took immediate, bold action to deliver relief to the American people. The President proposed and signed into law the American Rescue Plan Act of 2021 (the American Rescue Plan)—a historic, comprehensive package designed to help change the course of the COVID-19 pandemic, deliver desperately needed support to millions of workers, families, and small businesses, and build a bridge to a robust, equitable economic recovery.

The American Rescue Plan advanced three critical priorities. First, it included urgently needed resources to help families and businesses weather the worst of the COVID-19 pandemic, including: $1,400 per-person rescue payments for households across America; extended unemployment insurance; housing and nutrition assistance; increased access to safe and reliable child care and affordable healthcare; historic expansions of middle class tax relief for working families; a solution to the crisis in America's multi-employer pension system; and support for hard-hit small businesses. Second, it provided vital resources to help safely reopen K-8 schools in communities across the Nation and address the needs of students. Third, it provided resources to help mount an unprecedented Government-wide effort to defeat the COVID-19 pandemic, including funding to: set up community vaccination sites nationwide; dramatically scale up testing and tracing; eliminate supply shortage problems; support community health centers; and address health disparities.

The resources included in the American Rescue Plan, coupled with the President's whole-of-Government response, have already begun to change the course of the COVID-19 pandemic and bolster the economy. In a matter of months, the Administration turned the slow-moving and underperforming vaccination effort it inherited into one of the most effective vaccination systems anywhere in the world. The Administration exceeded the President's initial goal of administering 100 million shots in his first 100 days, ultimately administering 220 million shots in the President's first 100 days in office—an unprecedented national mobilization. As of May 17, nearly 60 percent of American adults had received at least one shot; nearly 85 percent of all seniors had received at least one shot and nearly 73 percent were fully vaccinated; and daily deaths were down more than 80 percent since January 20. All Americans 12 and older are now eligible for a COVID-19 vaccine. In addition, the Administration met the President's goal to reopen a majority of K-8 schools within the first 100 days.

As the Administration has ramped up the national COVID-19 pandemic response, the economy has started to get back on track. The President oversaw the creation of more than 1.5 million new jobs in his first 100 days in office—more than any president on record. Economists have raised their Gross Domestic Product growth forecasts for 2021 to 6.6 percent, which would be the fastest pace of economic growth in America in nearly four decades. Consumer confidence and spending are on the rise. Business activity is rebounding.

Moreover, the Administration is ensuring the American Rescue Plan reaches families, communities, and small businesses. The Department of the Treasury has already delivered more than 165 million relief payments of up to $1,400 per person. The American Rescue Plan is delivering nutrition assistance to millions of Americans facing hunger, rental assistance and mortgage relief to help families stay in their homes, and loans to small businesses to help keep their doors open. It includes the largest investment in child care since World War II, which will especially benefit women of color. It is reducing healthcare premiums, expanding access to insurance coverage, and addressing persistent health disparities. It ensures that millions of American workers and retirees will receive the pensions they earned. In addition,

it is projected to reduce poverty by 32 percent, lifting a total of nearly 13 million Americans out of poverty—this would mean a 38-percent drop in the Black poverty rate, a 43-percent drop in the Hispanic poverty rate, a 23-percent drop in the Asian American and Pacific Islander poverty rate, and a 50-percent drop in the child poverty rate.

Emerging from Crises and Focusing on the Future

While significant challenges remain, the American Rescue Plan has succeeded by virtually every measure in helping address the immediate economic and public health crises the Administration inherited. However, even as the Administration makes significant strides to get the Nation back on track, the President believes it is not enough to go back to the way things were before the COVID-19 pandemic struck, or to settle for a shrunken view of what America can be. The President believes this is a moment to build back better and to rise to meet the full range of challenges and opportunities before us—from rebuilding America's crumbling physical and care infrastructure and creating millions of good-paying jobs, to combatting climate change and revitalizing American manufacturing, to expanding access to both early childhood and higher education and addressing systemic inequities, and more.

None of this work will be easy. Many of the challenges America faces have been years or decades in the making. These challenges do not lend themselves to quick or easy solutions, nor will they be fully resolved in a single year or with a single budget. But it is precisely at the moments of greatest consequence that Americans have shown their capacity to think big and do the hard work of charting a new and better course for the future. Our charge now is to carry that legacy forward.

BUILDING BACK BETTER

Under the President's leadership, America is getting back on track. We have begun turning the tide on the pandemic. Our economy is growing and creating jobs. Students are getting back into classrooms. And we have shown yet again there is no quit in America. But our work has only begun.

For all of the hard-won progress our Nation has made in recent months, we cannot afford to simply return to the way things were before the pandemic and economic downturn, with the old economy's structural weaknesses and inequities still in place. We must seize this moment to reimagine and rebuild a new American economy—an economy that invests in the promise and potential of every single American; that leaves no one out and no one behind; and that makes it easier for families to break into the middle class and stay in the middle class.

The Budget details the President's proposals to advance that agenda this year. It includes the two historic plans the President has already put forward—the American Jobs Plan and the American Families Plan—and outlines a package of discretionary proposals to help restore core functions of Government and reinvest in the foundations of the Nation's strength. It also calls on the Congress to reduce prescription drug costs and expand and improve health coverage. Enacting the Budget policies into law this year would strengthen our Nation's economy and lay the foundation for shared prosperity, while also putting the Nation on a sound fiscal course. Importantly, even as the Administration pursues this historic agenda, the President also believes that there will be more to accomplish in the coming years. This year's Budget gives a full accounting of the first, critical steps our Nation must take to begin the work of building back better.

The American Jobs Plan

The Budget begins with the American Jobs Plan—an investment in America that would create millions of good jobs, rebuild the Nation's infrastructure, and position the United States to out-compete China. Public domestic investment as a share of the economy has fallen by more than 40 percent since the 1960s. The American Jobs Plan would invest in America in a way that has not occurred since the interstate highways were built and the Space Race was won.

The United States is the wealthiest Nation in the world, yet ranks 13th when it comes to the overall quality of the Nation's infrastructure. After decades of disinvestment, America's roads, bridges, and water systems are crumbling. The electric grid is vulnerable to catastrophic outages. Too many lack access to affordable, high-speed internet and to quality housing. The past year has led to job losses and threatened economic security, eroding more than 30 years of progress in women's labor force participation. It has unmasked the fragility of America's caregiving infrastructure. In addition, the Nation is falling behind its biggest competitors in research and development (R&D), manufacturing, and training. It has never been more important to invest in strengthening the Nation's infrastructure and competitiveness, and in creating the good-paying, union jobs of the future.

As with great projects of the past, the President's plan would unify and mobilize the Nation to meet the great challenges of our time: the climate crisis and the ambitions of an autocratic China. It would invest in Americans and deliver the jobs and opportunities they deserve. Unlike past major investments, the plan prioritizes addressing long-standing and persistent racial injustice. The plan targets 40 percent of the benefits of climate and clean infrastructure investments to disadvantaged communities. In addition, the plan invests in rural communities and communities impacted by the market-based transition to clean energy. Specifically, the President's plan:

Fixes Highways, Rebuilds Bridges, and Upgrades Ports, Airports, and Transit Systems. The President's plan would: modernize 20,000 miles of highways, roads, and mainstreets; fix the 10 most economically significant bridges in the Nation in need of reconstruction; repair the worst 10,000 smaller bridges, providing critical linkages to communities; replace thousands of buses and rail cars; repair hundreds of stations; renew airports; modernize ports of entry; and expand transit and rail into new communities.

Delivers Clean Drinking Water, a Renewed Electric Grid, and High-Speed Broadband to All Americans. The President's plan would eliminate all lead pipes and service lines in drinking water systems, improving the health of the Nation's children and communities of color. It would put hundreds of thousands of people to work laying thousands of miles of transmission lines and capping hundreds of thousands of orphan oil and gas wells and abandoned mines. It would also bring affordable, reliable, high-speed broadband to every household, including the more than 35 percent of rural families who lack access to broadband infrastructure, the millions of families paying too much for broadband, and the millions of low-income and marginalized communities left behind by digital redlining and the digital divide.

Builds, Preserves, and Retrofits More than Two Million Homes and Commercial Buildings, Modernizes the Nation's Schools and Child Care Facilities, and Upgrades Veterans' Hospitals and Federal Buildings. The President's plan would create good jobs by building, rehabilitating, and retrofitting affordable, accessible, energy efficient, and resilient housing, commercial buildings, schools, and child care facilities all over the Nation while also vastly improving the Nation's Federal facilities, especially those that serve veterans.

Solidifies the Infrastructure of America's Care Economy by Creating Jobs and Raising Wages and Benefits for Essential Home Care Workers. These workers—the majority of whom are women of color—have been underpaid and undervalued for too long. The President's plan makes substantial investments in the infrastructure of America's care economy, starting by creating new and better jobs for caregiving workers. It would provide home and community-based care for individuals who otherwise would need to wait as many as five years to get the services they badly need. The President also looks forward to working with the Congress on other policies to improve economic security and access to healthcare for seniors and people with disabilities.

Revitalizes Manufacturing, Secures U.S. Supply Chains, Invests in R&D, and Trains Americans for the Jobs of the Future. The President's plan would ensure that the best, diverse minds in America are put to work creating the innovations of the future while creating hundreds of thousands of quality jobs today. American workers would build and make things in every part of the Nation, and they would be trained for well-paying, middle-class jobs using evidence-based approaches such as sector-based training and registered apprenticeships.

Creates Good-Quality Jobs that Pay Prevailing Wages in Safe and Healthy Workplaces while Ensuring Workers Have a Free and Fair Choice to Organize, Join a

Union, and Bargain Collectively with Their Employers. To ensure that American taxpayers' dollars benefit working families and their communities, and not multinational corporations or foreign governments, the plan requires that goods and materials are made in America and shipped on U.S.-flag, U.S.-crewed vessels. The plan also would ensure that Americans, especially those who have endured systemic discrimination and exclusion for generations, finally have a fair shot at obtaining good-paying jobs with: a choice to join a union; higher and equal pay; safe and healthy workplaces; and workplaces free from racial, gender, and other forms of discrimination and harassment.

Restructures the Corporate Tax Code to Ensure that Wealthy Corporations Pay Their Fair Share and Invest Here at Home. Alongside the American Jobs Plan, the President has put forward a Made in America tax plan that would reward investment at home, stop profit shifting, and ensure other nations would not gain a competitive edge by becoming tax havens. The key components of the Made in America tax plan include a 28-percent corporate tax rate and a global minimum tax alongside a strong incentive for other countries to enact reasonable minimum taxes as well. The plan also includes measures to prevent corporate inversions and offshoring, as well as a new minimum tax on corporate book income to ensure that massive, profitable companies can no longer get away with paying no Federal income tax. In addition, the plan also eliminates tax preferences for fossil fuels. This is a generational opportunity to fundamentally shift how countries around the world tax corporations so that big corporations cannot escape or eliminate the taxes they owe by offshoring jobs and profits.

The American Families Plan

To complement the American Jobs Plan and help extend the benefits of economic growth to all Americans, the Budget also includes the American Families Plan—a historic investment to: help families cover the basic expenses that so many struggle with now; lower health insurance premiums; and continue the historic reductions in child poverty in the American Rescue Plan Act of 2021 (American Rescue Plan). Together, these plans reinvest in the future of the American economy and American workers and would help the Nation out-compete China and other countries around the world. Specifically, the President's American Families Plan:

Adds at Least Four Years of Free Education. Investing in education is a down payment on the future of America. As access to high school became more widely available at the turn of the 20th Century, it made America the best-educated and best-prepared Nation in the world. Yet, everyone knows that 12 years is not enough today. The American Families Plan would make transformational investments from early childhood to postsecondary education so that all children and young people are able to grow, learn, and gain the skills they need to succeed. It would provide universal access to high-quality pre-school to all three- and four-year-olds, led by a well-trained and well-compensated workforce. It would provide Americans two years of free community college. It would invest in making college more affordable for low- and middle-income students, including students at Historically Black Colleges and Universities (HBCUs), Tribal Colleges and Universities (TCUs), and Minority-Serving Institutions (MSIs) such as Hispanic-Serving Institutions (HSIs) and Asian American and Native American Pacific Islander-Serving Institutions. It would also invest in America's teachers and students, improving teacher training and support so that schools become engines of growth at every level.

Provides Direct Support to Children and Families. The Nation is strongest when everyone has the opportunity to join the workforce and contribute to the economy. However, many workers struggle to both hold a full-time job and care for themselves and their families. The American Families Plan would provide direct support to families to ensure that low- and middle-income families spend no more than seven percent of their income on child care, and that the child care they access is of high-quality and provided by a well-trained and well-compensated child care workforce. It would also provide direct support to workers and families by creating a national comprehensive paid family and medical leave program that would bring the American system in line with competitor nations that offer paid leave programs. A comprehensive paid family and medical leave program would allow workers to take the time they need to bond with a new child, to care for their own serious illness, and to care for a seriously ill loved one. The system would also allow people to manage their health and the health of their families. The plan would also make investments to improve maternal health and provide critical nutrition assistance to families who need it most and expand access to healthy meals to the Nation's students—dramatically reducing childhood hunger.

Extends Tax Cuts for Families with Children and American Workers. While the American Rescue Plan provided critical help to hundreds of millions of Americans, too many families and workers feel the squeeze of too-low wages and the high costs of meeting their basic needs and aspirations. At the same time, the wealthiest Americans continue to get further and further ahead. The American Families Plan would extend key tax cuts in the American Rescue Plan that benefit lower- and middle-income workers and families, including the expansions of the Child Tax Credit, the Earned Income Tax Credit, and the Child and Dependent Care Tax Credit. In addition to making it easier for families to make ends meet, tax credits for working families have been shown to boost child academic and economic performance over time. The American Families Plan would also extend the expanded health insurance tax credits in the American Rescue Plan. These credits are providing premium relief that is lowering health insurance costs by an average of $50 per person per month for more than nine million people, and would enable millions of uninsured people to gain coverage.

Leading economic research has shown that the investments proposed in the American Families Plan would yield significant economic returns—boosting productivity and economic growth,

producing a larger, more productive, and healthier workforce on a sustained basis, and generating savings to States and the Federal Government. A recent review indicates that every dollar invested in early childhood programs resulted in an estimated range of $2.50 to $10.80 in benefits as children grew up healthier, were more likely to graduate high school and college, and earned more as adults. A 2020 study by Nobel Laureate James Heckman found that every dollar invested in a high-quality, birth until age five program for the most economically disadvantaged children resulted in $7.30 in benefits. Paid leave has been shown to keep mothers in the workforce, increasing labor force participation and boosting economic growth. In addition, sustained tax credits for families with children have been found to yield a lifetime of benefits, ranging from higher educational attainment to higher lifetime earnings.

Supports Tax Reform that Rewards Work— Not Wealth. The American Families Plan also includes commonsense reforms to the income tax code that would rebalance the tax system away from special preferences for wealth and toward fair treatment regardless of the type of income. The President's tax agenda would not only reverse some of the biggest 2017 tax law giveaways, but would reform the tax code so that the wealthy have to play by the same rules as everyone else. It would ensure that high-income Americans pay the tax they owe under the law—ending the unfair system of enforcement that collects almost all taxes due on wages, while regularly collecting a smaller share of business and capital income. The plan would also eliminate long-standing loopholes, including lower taxes on capital gains and dividends for the wealthy, which reward wealth over work. Importantly, these reforms would also rein in the ways that the tax code widens racial disparities in income and wealth.

Reinvesting in the Foundations of the Nation's Strength

The American Jobs Plan and the American Families Plan represent once-in-a-generation investments in the Nation's future that would create jobs, grow the middle class, and expand the benefits of economic growth to all Americans. To truly build back better, the Nation must also begin to reinvest in core functions of Government and the foundations of the Nation's strength—and that is exactly what the Budget does.

Over the past decade, due in large measure to overly restrictive budget caps, the Nation significantly underinvested in crucial public services, benefits, and protections. Since 2010, non-defense discretionary funding has shrunk significantly as a share of the economy.

The consequences of this broad disinvestment are plain to see. Anticipating, preparing for, and fighting a global pandemic requires a robust public health infrastructure. Yet, going into the COVID-19 pandemic, funding for the Centers for Disease Control and Prevention (CDC) was 10 percent lower than a decade ago, adjusted for inflation. Creating an economy that works for everyone—including rural, urban, and tribal communities—requires investments in working families who drive growth and prosperity. However, the Government has chronically underinvested in crucial programs such as Head Start, which serves 95,000 fewer children today than it did a decade ago. Responding to the climate crisis

depends on helping communities transition to a cleaner future. Instead of investing in climate science and technology at the Environmental Protection Agency (EPA), funding has been reduced by 27 percent since 2010, adjusted for inflation.

The President believes now is the time to begin reversing this trend—and the expiration of nearly a decade of budget caps presents a unique opportunity to do so. That is why the Budget includes targeted discretionary investments across a range of key areas—from improving America's public health infrastructure and improving education, to tackling the climate crisis and fostering economic growth and security, to restoring America's global standing and confronting 21st Century security challenges.

Overall, the Budget would restore non-defense discretionary funding to 3.3 percent of Gross Domestic Product, roughly equal to the historical average over the last 30 years, while providing robust funding for national defense as well as for other instruments of national power—including diplomacy, development, and economic statecraft—that enhance the effectiveness of national defense spending and promote national security.

EXPANDING OPPORTUNITY

The American Jobs Plan and the American Families Plan would boost worker productivity, invest in American ingenuity, create good-paying jobs, and provide real opportunity and security for millions of families. Those plans are complemented by the Budget's additional foundational investments. Together, this suite of policies would contribute to a stronger, more inclusive economy over the long term by: advancing economic dignity, equity, and security for all Americans; expanding opportunity; and creating good-paying jobs.

Improving Education

Makes Historic Investments in High-Poverty Schools. Addressing entrenched disparities

in education is both a moral and economic imperative. That is why the Budget proposes a historic $36.5 billion investment in Title I grants, a $20 billion increase from the 2021 enacted level. This investment would provide under-resourced schools with the funding needed to deliver a high-quality education to all of their students by ensuring teachers at Title I schools are paid competitively, providing equitable access to a rigorous curriculum, increasing access to preschool, and providing meaningful incentives for States to examine and address inequalities in school funding systems.

Expands Access to Affordable Early Child Care and Learning. To lay the foundation for the major long-term investments in the American Families Plan, the Budget includes $7.4 billion for the Child Care and Development Block Grant, an increase of $1.5 billion from the 2021 enacted level, to expand access to quality, affordable child care for families across the Nation, as well as an $11.9 billion investment in Head Start, a $1.2 billion increase, which would ensure more children start kindergarten ready to learn on day one. The Administration would also work with States to ensure that these resources support increased wages for early educators and family child care providers, the majority of whom are women of color.

Boosts Support for Children with Disabilities. To ensure that children with disabilities have the opportunity to thrive, the Budget includes $16 billion, a $2.7 billion increase from the 2021 enacted level, for Individuals with Disabilities Education Act (IDEA) grants that would support special education and related services for more than 7.6 million preschool through grade 12 students. This is a significant first step toward fully funding IDEA. The Budget also provides $732 million for early intervention services for infants and toddlers with disabilities or delays, funding services that have a proven record of improving academic and developmental outcomes. The $250 million increase for early intervention services would be paired with reforms to expand access to these services for underserved children, including children of color and children from low-income families.

Prioritizes the Physical and Mental Well-Being of Students. Recognizing the profound effect of physical and mental health on academic achievement, the Budget provides $1 billion in addition to the resources in the American Rescue Plan, to increase the number of counselors, nurses, and mental health professionals in schools. In addition, the Budget provides $443 million for Full Service Community Schools, which play a critical role in providing comprehensive wrap-around services to students and their families, from afterschool programs, to adult education opportunities, to health and nutrition services.

Increases Pell Grants and Expands Institutional and Student Supports. The Budget provides discretionary funding to increase the maximum Pell Grant by $400—the largest one-time increase since 2009. This increase, together with the $1,475 Pell Grant increase in the American Families Plan, represents a significant first step to deliver on the President's goal to double the grant. The Budget also increases discretionary funding, and provides funding first proposed under the American Families Plan, to expand institutional and student supports at community colleges, HBCUs, TCUs, and MSIs. The Administration also looks forward to working with the Congress on changes to the Higher Education Act of 1965 that ease the burden of student debt, including through improvements to the Income Driven Repayment and Public Service Loan Forgiveness programs.

Advancing Dignity, Equity, and Security

Expands Opportunities for Minority-Owned Businesses. To help address longstanding racial inequity and eliminate barriers for minority-owned firms, the Budget includes $70 million, an increase of $22 million, to fund investments in economic development grants and research to ensure policies effectively support the minority business community. In addition, the Budget provides $330 million, an increase of 22.2 percent above the 2021 enacted level, to support expanding the role of Community Development Financial Institutions (CDFIs), which offer loans to start-ups and small businesses to promote the production of affordable housing and community revitalization projects. This investment builds on an unprecedented level of support for the CDFI industry in 2021, including more than $3 billion in direct funding, $9 billion for investments in depository and credit union CDFIs and Minority Depository Institutions, and provisions in the American Rescue Plan encouraging CDFI participation in the $10 billion State Small Business Credit Initiative.

Increases Rural Outreach and Connectivity. The Budget provides $32 million for a renewed and expanded initiative, StrikeForce, to help people in high poverty rural communities tap into Federal resources. The Budget also provides an increase of $65 million from the 2021 enacted level for the Rural e-Connectivity Program "Reconnect" for rural broadband. The Budget also includes $318 million for regional commissions, which provide economic development assistance in distressed, rural communities through infrastructure investments, workforce development, and other activities.

Spurs Infrastructure Modernization and Rehabilitation in Marginalized Communities. The Budget provides $3.8 billion for the Community Development Block Grant program, which includes a targeted increase of $295 million for the modernization and rehabilitation of public infrastructure and facilities, such as recreational centers and commercial corridor improvements, in historically underfunded and marginalized communities facing persistent poverty.

Supports Transportation Equity. The Budget includes significant funding for major discretionary competitive grant programs, including Rebuilding American Infrastructure with Sustainability and Equity transit Capital Investment Grants, and Port Infrastructure Development grants. In addition, the Budget invests in rail as a down-payment to the President's commitment to passenger rail. The Budget also proposes $110 million for a new Thriving Communities initiative, which would foster transportation equity by providing capacity building grants to underserved communities. These programs would ensure that more communities have cleaner, robust, and affordable transportation options, including high-quality transit, equitable transit-oriented development, and other enhancements to improve neighborhood quality of life and address climate change.

Ensures Workers' Health, Safety, and Rights Are Protected. The Budget provides increased funding to the worker protection agencies in the Department of Labor to ensure workers are treated with dignity and respect in the workplace.

The Administration is also committed to ending the abusive practice of misclassifying employees as independent contractors, which deprives these workers of critical protections and benefits. In addition to including funding in the Budget for stronger enforcement, the Administration intends to work with the Congress to develop comprehensive legislation to strengthen and extend protections against misclassification across appropriate Federal statutes.

Strengthens the Unemployment Insurance System. The COVID-19 pandemic triggered an economic crisis that has left millions of Americans relying on unemployment insurance and exposed major flaws and gaps in how the system is administered. To correct for these weaknesses and address chronic delays, the Budget includes significant support to modernize and improve States' administration of the program and to help unemployed workers return to work, building on investments included in the American Rescue Plan and setting the stage for broad changes to modernize the program. This includes reforming the unemployment insurance system so it provides adequate benefits in every State, automatically responds to downturns, reflects the modern economy and labor force, uses more equitable and progressive financing mechanisms, and provides expanded reemployment services. Reform must also ensure that unemployment insurance benefits are both more accessible and less vulnerable to fraud, including from sophisticated criminal rings.

Advances Equity in Child Welfare. The Budget proposes $100 million in new competitive grants to advance racial equity in the child welfare system and reduce unnecessary child removals. The Budget also increases funding for State and local child abuse prevention programs by over 30 percent compared to the 2021 enacted level. The Administration is also interested in working with the Congress to enact further child welfare reforms that advance equity, improve children's well-being, and ensure all children, birth families, and prospective kinship, foster, and adoptive parents are served equitably and with dignity.

Expanding Housing Opportunity and Reducing the Racial Wealth Gap

Extends Housing Vouchers to 200,000 More Families. At a time when millions of families are struggling to pay their rent or mortgage, the Budget proposes to provide $30.4 billion for Housing Choice Vouchers, expanding vital housing assistance to 200,000 more families with a focus on those who are homeless or fleeing domestic violence. The President looks forward to working with the Congress to build on this investment and achieve the long-term goal of providing housing vouchers to all eligible households, while increasing the program's impact on equity and poverty alleviation.

Accelerates Efforts to End Homelessness. The Budget builds on important provisions included in the American Rescue Plan by providing a $500 million increase for Homeless Assistance Grants to support more than 100,000 households—including survivors of domestic violence and homeless youth, helping prevent and reduce homelessness.

Enhances Household Mobility and Neighborhood Choice. In addition to expanding the Housing Choice Voucher program to serve 200,000 more families, the Budget includes funding for mobility-related supportive services to provide low-income families who live in concentrated areas of poverty with greater options to move to higher-opportunity neighborhoods.

Supports Access to Homeownership and Pandemic Relief. The Budget supports access to homeownership for underserved borrowers through the Federal Housing Administration's (FHA) mortgage insurance programs. FHA is a crucial source of mortgage financing for first-time and minority homebuyers, who accounted for 83 percent and 37 percent, respectively, of FHA home purchase loans in 2020. In addition, through its expanded and streamlined loss mitigation program, FHA continues to provide urgent relief to homeowners suffering financially due to the COVID-19 pandemic.

Invests in Affordable Housing in Tribal Communities. Native Americans are seven times more likely to live in overcrowded conditions and five times more likely to have plumbing, kitchen, or heating problems than all U.S. households. The Budget helps address the poor housing conditions in tribal areas by providing $900 million to fund tribal efforts to expand affordable housing, improve housing conditions and infrastructure, and increase economic opportunities for low-income families.

Creating Jobs and Growth—Now and for the Future

Supports a Future Made in America. The President is committed to ensuring the future is made in America by all of America's workers. The American Jobs Plan proposes transformative new funding for manufacturing programs at the National Institute of Standards and Technology (NIST), and the Budget complements those investments with additional discretionary funding, enabling the establishment of two new Manufacturing Innovation Institutes, in addition to institutes previously launched by the Departments of Defense (DOD) and Energy (DOE). The Budget also nearly doubles funding for the Manufacturing Extension Partnership to boost the competitiveness of small and medium manufacturers.

Renews America's Commitment to R&D. The Budget proposes historic increases in funding for foundational R&D across a range of scientific agencies—including the National Science Foundation (NSF), the National Aeronautics and Space Administration (NASA), DOE, NIST, and others—to help spur innovation across the economy and renew America's global leadership. These investments would: accelerate discoveries that would transform America's understanding of the solar system and universe; launch the next generation of satellites to study and improve life on Earth; and support upgrades to cutting-edge scientific user facilities at DOE national laboratories to build climate and clean energy research programs and train the next generation of scientists at HBCUs and MSIs. This funding, combined with the investments proposed as part of the American Jobs Plan, would firmly reestablish the United States as a global leader in R&D.

Committing to Criminal Justice Reform and Redressing Longstanding Injustice

Reforms the Federal Criminal Justice System. The Budget supports key investments in First Step Act of 2018 (FSA) implementation, advancing the provision of high-quality substance use disorder treatment, reentry services, and recidivism reduction programming. Building on the bipartisan FSA, the Budget also incorporates savings from prison population reduction measures that prioritize incarceration alternatives for low-risk offenders.

Invests in Community Policing, Police Reform, and Other Efforts to Address Systemic Inequities. The Administration will take bold action to root out systemic inequities in the Nation's justice system. In addition to investing in programs that support community-oriented policing and practices, the Budget also proposes to expand grants that support efforts to reform State and local criminal justice systems, including funding to support juvenile justice programs, drug courts and alternative court programs, public defenders, and Second Chance Act of 2007 programs.

Invests in Civil Rights Offices across Government. The Budget supports significant increases for civil rights offices and activities across Federal agencies to ensure that the Nation's laws are enforced fairly and equitably.

Promotes State and Local Efforts to Prevent and Redress Housing Discrimination. The Budget provides $85 million in grants to support State and local fair housing enforcement organizations and to further education, outreach, and training on rights and responsibilities under Federal fair housing laws. The Budget also invests in the Department of Housing and Urban Development (HUD) staff and operations capacity to deliver on the President's housing priorities, including commitments outlined in the Presidential Memorandum on Redressing Our Nation's and the Federal Government's History of Discriminatory Housing Practices and Policies.

Makes Major Investments in Environmental Justice. For decades, low-income and marginalized communities have been overburdened with air pollution and other environmental hazards. The Budget includes a 44-percent increase in funding for EPA's Brownfields program, which would enable States to clean up contaminated properties and assist them in turning idle properties into hubs for economic revitalization. The Budget provides $400 million for HUD's Lead Hazard and Healthy Homes grants, which enable State and local governments and nonprofits to reduce lead-based paint and other health hazards in the homes of low-income families with young children. The Budget provides $5 million to the Department of Justice (DOJ) to allow the Environment and Natural Resources Division to increase affirmative casework related to environmental justice.

INVESTING IN PUBLIC HEALTH INFRASTRUCTURE

The United States faces no more urgent task than defeating the COVID-19 pandemic. That is why the American Rescue Plan included vital funding to set up community vaccination sites nationwide, scale up testing and tracing, reduce supply shortage problems, support community health centers, address health disparities, and safely reopen schools. The Budget builds on this foundation by proposing investments to build a healthier, more resilient Nation over the long term, including funding to ensure the Nation is better positioned to prevent and respond to future public health crises, help defeat other diseases and epidemics, and invest in cutting-edge medical research.

Strengthening Public Health Infrastructure and Meeting Crisis-Related Needs

Improves Readiness for Future Public Health Crises. The Budget includes $8.7 billion in discretionary funding for CDC—the largest budget authority increase in nearly two decades—to restore capacity at the world's preeminent public health agency. Building on the investments in the American Rescue Plan, CDC would use this additional funding to support core public health capacity improvements in States and Territories, modernize public health data collection nationwide, train new epidemiologists and other public health experts, and rebuild international capacity to detect, prepare for, and respond to emerging global threats.

Expands Access to Mental Healthcare. The COVID-19 pandemic has helped expose the strain on the Nation's mental healthcare system and the need for additional sustained resources. The Budget builds on mental health resources included in the American Rescue Plan by: calling for historic investments, including $1.6 billion, more than double the 2021 enacted level, for the Community Mental Health Services Block Grant; additional funding to support the needs of those who are involved in the criminal justice system; resources to partner mental health providers with law enforcement; and funds to expand suicide prevention activities.

Invests in Efforts to End Gender-Based Violence. The COVID-19 pandemic has exacerbated domestic violence and sexual assault and has compounded the barriers to safety and economic security, creating a "shadow pandemic" for many women and girls who are largely confined to their home with their abuser. To help address this growing crisis, the Budget provides $1 billion for DOJ Violence Against Women Act of 1994 programs, nearly double the 2021 level, including funding for new programs to expand restorative justice efforts, protect transgender survivors, and support women at HBCUs, HSIs, and TCUs to ensure these institutions have the same resources as other schools to address this pervasive issue.

The Budget also provides a significant increase in funding at the Department of Health and Human Services (HHS) for domestic violence shelters and community-based programs, hotlines, cash assistance for survivors, medical support, and integrated healthcare services. The Administration also looks forward to working with the Congress to expand the new cash assistance program for survivors of domestic violence by providing additional resources beyond 2022.

Promotes Health Equity for American Indians and Alaska Natives. To begin redressing long-standing, stark health inequities experienced by American Indians and Alaska Natives, the Budget proposes to dramatically increase funding for the Indian Health Service (IHS) by $2.2 billion. In addition, to ensure a more predictable funding stream for IHS, the Budget for the first time includes an advance appropriation for IHS in 2023.

Addresses Racial Disparities in Healthcare. Building on efforts in the American Rescue Plan to advance equity and reduce health disparities in all healthcare programs, the Budget includes additional funding to expand access to culturally competent care. The Budget also includes $153 million for CDC's Social Determinants of Health program to support States and Territories in improving health equity and data collection for racial and ethnic populations. The Administration also looks forward to working with the Congress to advance the President's goal of doubling the Federal investment in community health centers, which would help reduce health disparities by expanding access to care.

Reduces Maternal Mortality Rate and Ends Race-Based Disparities in Maternal Mortality. The United States has the highest maternal mortality rate among developed nations, with an unacceptably high mortality rate for Black, American Indian/Alaska Native, and other women of color. To help end this high rate of maternal mortality and race-based disparities in outcomes among birthing people—and in addition to the investment in maternal health included in the American Families Plan—the

Budget includes more than $200 million to: reduce maternal mortality and morbidity rates nationwide; bolster Maternal Mortality Review Committees; expand the Rural Maternity and Obstetrics Management Strategies program; help cities place early childhood development experts in pediatrician offices with a high percentage of Medicaid and Children's Health Insurance Program patients; implement implicit bias training for healthcare providers; and create State pregnancy medical home programs.

Defeating Other Diseases and Epidemics

Launches Advanced Research Projects Agency for Health (ARPA-H). The Budget includes a major investment of $6.5 billion to launch ARPA-H, which would provide significant increases in direct Federal R&D spending in health. With an initial focus on cancer and other diseases such as diabetes and Alzheimer's, this major investment in Federal R&D would drive transformational innovation in health research and speed application and implementation of health breakthroughs. This funding is part of a $51 billion request for the National Institutes of Health (NIH) to continue to support research that enhances health, lengthens life, and reduces illness and disability.

Makes a Major Investment to Help End the Opioid Epidemic. The opioid epidemic has shattered families, claimed lives, and ravaged communities across the Nation—and the COVID-19 pandemic has only deepened this crisis. That is why the Budget includes a historic investment of $10.7 billion in discretionary funding in HHS, an increase of $3.9 billion over the 2021 enacted level, to support research, prevention, treatment, and recovery support services, with targeted investments to support populations with unique needs, including Native Americans, older Americans, and rural populations. The Budget also includes $621 million specific to the Department of Veterans Affairs' (VA's) Opioid

Prevention and Treatment programs, including programs in support of the Jason Simcakoski Memorial and Promise Act.

Combats the Gun Violence Public Health Epidemic. The Budget includes $2.1 billion, an increase of $232 million above the 2021 enacted level, for DOJ to address the gun violence public health crisis plaguing communities across the Nation. Investments include $401 million in State and local grants, an increase of $162 million or 68 percent. This level supports existing programs to improve background check systems, and invests in new programs to incentivize State adoption of gun licensing laws and establish voluntary gun buyback pilot programs. In addition, a total of $1.6 billion is provided to the Bureau of Alcohol, Tobacco, Firearms, and Explosives, an increase of $70 million or five percent over the 2021 enacted level, to oversee the safe sale, storage, and ownership of firearms and to support the Agency's other work to fight violent crime. The Budget request for HHS doubles funding for firearm violence prevention research at CDC and NIH. Combined, the Budget includes $200 million in discretionary resources for DOJ and HHS to support a new Community Violence Intervention initiative to implement evidence-based community violence interventions locally, which may include hospital-based interventions. In addition to these amounts, the Budget supports the American Jobs Plan proposal for $5 billion in total mandatory resources from 2023 to 2029 to provide long-term support for the Community Violence Intervention initiative.

Commits to Ending the HIV/AIDS Epidemic. To help accelerate and strengthen efforts to end the HIV/AIDS epidemic in the United States, the Budget includes $670 million within HHS to help aggressively reduce new HIV cases while increasing access to treatment, expanding the use of pre-exposure prophylaxis, also known as PrEP, and ensuring equitable access to services and supports.

TACKLING THE CLIMATE CRISIS

Climate change is one of the greatest challenges of our time. It is also an opportunity to create new industries and good-paying jobs with a free and fair choice to join a union, revitalize America's energy communities and the economy, and position America as the world's clean energy superpower. In addition to the American Jobs Plan, the Budget includes more than $36 billion of investments to combat climate change—an increase of more than $14 billion compared to 2021—by investing in resilience and clean energy, enhancing U.S. competitiveness, and putting America on a path to achieve net-zero emissions no later than 2050—all while supporting communities that have been left behind and ensuring that 40 percent of the benefits from tackling the climate crisis are targeted toward addressing the disproportionately high cumulative impacts on disadvantaged communities.

Building Clean Energy Projects and Investing in Resilience

Improves Energy Efficiency, Safety, and Resilience of Low-Income Homes and Public Buildings. The Budget invests $1.7 billion in energy saving retrofits to homes, schools, and Federal buildings. This investment includes $800 million in new investments across HUD programs for rehabilitation and modernization to further climate resilience and energy efficiency, which would lower the costs and improve the quality of public and HUD-assisted housing, and $400 million at DOE for the weatherization of low-income homes.

Creates Good-Paying Jobs Building Clean Energy Projects. Transforming the U.S. electricity sector—and electrifying an increasing share of the economy—represents one of the biggest job creation and economic opportunity engines of the 21st Century. That is why the Budget provides $2 billion to put welders, electricians, and other skilled laborers to work building clean energy projects across the Nation. This investment supports a historic energy efficiency and clean electricity standard that would transform the electric sector to be carbon-pollution free by 2035 while creating good-paying union jobs.

Invests in Climate Resilience and Disaster Planning. The Budget provides $815 million—a $540 million increase above the 2021 enacted level—to incorporate climate impacts into pre-disaster planning and projects to ensure that the Nation is rebuilding smarter and safer for the future. The Budget also provides more than $1.2 billion above the 2021 enacted level to increase the resilience of ecosystems and communities across the Nation to wildfires, flooding, and drought, including an additional $100 million for CDC's Climate and Health program. Consistent with the President's national conservation goal and the America the Beautiful initiative, the Budget also makes critical investments to help communities conserve important lands and waters, expand access to the outdoors for underserved communities, and deploy natural solutions to climate change.

Helps Tribal Nations Address the Climate Crisis. Tribal communities are particularly vulnerable to the impacts of climate change, which threatens their cultural and economic well-being. The Budget provides an increase of more than $450 million to facilitate climate mitigation, resilience, adaptation, and environmental justice projects in Indian Country, including investment to begin the process of transitioning tribal colleges to renewable energy.

Increases Demand for American Made, Zero-Emission Vehicles through Federal Procurement. To provide an immediate, clear, and stable source of demand to help accelerate American industrial capacity to produce clean vehicles and components, the Budget includes $600 million for electric vehicles and charging infrastructure in the individual budgets of 18 Federal agencies, including dedicated funds at the General Services Administration for other agencies and for the United States Postal Service charging infrastructure. This discretionary investment is one component of an overarching effort—combined with funding in the American

Jobs Plan—to leverage Federal procurement to create good-paying union jobs, and enable a clean transportation future.

Helping Communities Left Behind

Makes the Largest Investment in Environmental Justice in History. To support marginalized and overburdened communities across the Nation, the Budget invests more than $1.4 billion, including $936 million toward a new Accelerating Environmental and Economic Justice initiative at EPA. The initiative would create good-paying union jobs, clean up pollution, and secure environmental justice for communities that have been left behind. In order to hold polluters accountable, the initiative includes $100 million to develop a new community air quality monitoring and notification program, which would provide real-time data in the places with the highest levels of exposure to pollution.

Propels an Effort to Create 250,000 Jobs Remediating Abandoned Wells and Mines. The Budget includes over $580 million to remediate thousands of abandoned oil and gas wells and reclaim abandoned mines. This more than triples the current annual discretionary funding, building on the President's commitment to create 250,000 good-paying union jobs for skilled technicians and operators in some of the hardest hit communities in the Nation, while cleaning up hazardous sites. In line with the stated goals of this Administration, the Budget more than doubles funding for the Economic Development Administration's (EDA) Assistance to Coal Communities program. EDA's efforts are part of the work of the new Interagency Working Group on Coal and Power Plant Communities and Economic Revitalization, and complement other targeted investments across the Federal Government to help spur economic revitalization, create jobs, and support workers in hard-hit coal, oil and gas, and power plant communities.

Creates Jobs Improving Critical Water Infrastructure. Clean, safe drinking water should be a right in all communities—rural and urban, rich and poor. That is why the American

Jobs Plan would replace every lead service line in America. The Budget also includes significant funding—$3.6 billion—that could be used to advance water infrastructure improvement efforts for community water systems, schools, and households. These water infrastructure improvement efforts include repairing up to 180,000 septic systems, as well as broader efforts to improve drinking water and waste water infrastructure, while creating good-paying construction jobs that pay at least the prevailing wage across the Nation and in tribal communities.

Partners with Rural America to Grow Rural Economies and Tackle Rural Poverty. The Budget includes a number of proposals to invest in and create opportunities for rural Americans. This includes more than $300 million in new investments in the next generation of agriculture and conservation, including support for voluntary private lands conservation as part of the America the Beautiful initiative, renewable energy grants and loans, and the creation of a Civilian Climate Corps to create a new pathway to good-paying jobs in rural America. The Budget also supports $6.5 billion in lending to support additional clean energy, energy storage, and transmission projects in rural communities.

Increasing Competitiveness through Investments in Innovation and Science

Advances Climate Science and Sustainability Research. The Budget proposes over $4 billion to fund a broad portfolio of research across multiple agencies including the Department of the Interior, NASA, NSF, and others to improve understanding of the changing climate and inform adaptation and resilience measures.

Spurs Innovation in Clean Energy Technologies. The Budget invests more than $10 billion—a nearly 30-percent increase over 2021—in clean energy innovation across non-defense agencies. These investments would help transform the Nation's electric, transportation, buildings, and industrial sectors to achieve a net-zero carbon economy by 2050.

Drives Breakthrough Solutions in Climate Innovation. The Budget includes a total of $1 billion to create a new Advanced Research Projects Agency for Climate and invests in the existing Advanced Research Projects Agency-Energy. Together, these initiatives would support high-risk, high-reward solutions for adaptation, mitigation, and resilience against the climate crisis and enable robust investments in clean energy technology R&D.

Expands Observations, Research, and Climate Services. The Budget includes $7 billion for the National Oceanic and Atmospheric Administration (NOAA), an increase of $1.5 billion from the 2021 enacted level. These additional funds would allow NOAA to: expand its climate observation and forecasting work and provide better data and information to decisionmakers; support coastal resilience programs that would help protect communities from the economic and environmental impacts of climate change; and invest in modern infrastructure to enable these critical efforts.

Leading the World toward Achieving the Objectives of the Paris Agreement on Climate

Supports Global Emissions Reductions. To accelerate progress toward the Paris Agreement targets, the Budget includes a $1.2 billion contribution to the Green Climate Fund—the first American contribution since 2017—to help developing countries reduce emissions and adapt to climate change. The Budget also proposes $485 million to support other multilateral climate initiatives, including $100 million for international climate adaptation programs. The Budget provides approximately $700 million for the Department of State and U.S. Agency for International Development to assist developing countries in adapting to climate disruptions, expanding clean energy production, and reducing landscape emissions.

CONFRONTING 21ST CENTURY SECURITY CHALLENGES

From the COVID-19 pandemic to climate change, from the growing ambitions of China to the many global threats to democracy, successfully addressing global challenges will require working alongside and in partnership with other nations. After years of neglect, the Budget makes critical investments in diplomacy and development that would restore the health and morale of the Nation's foreign policy institutions, as well as America's relationships with key partners and allies. Diplomacy would once again be a centerpiece of American foreign policy, and America would once again be a leader on the world stage.

Renews American Leadership and Mobilizes Global Action. The Budget proposes reinvesting in the Nation's diplomatic corps and providing funding to support U.S. commitments to the World Health Organization, the United Nations (UN) Population Fund, and the UN High Commissioner for Human Rights, while continuing to press for needed reforms. The Budget also provides $1 billion in foreign assistance to bring an end to the COVID-19 pandemic and expand global health security activities, including to establish Global Health Security Agenda capacity-building programs in additional nations and increase investments in crosscutting research and viral discovery programs to detect and stamp out future infectious disease outbreaks. These funds would also support a new health security financing mechanism, developed alongside U.S. partners and allies, to ensure global readiness to respond to the next outbreak. In addition, recognizing that no single nation can meet the challenge of climate change alone, the Budget provides $2.5 billion for international climate programs to help rally the world against this urgent threat, restore U.S. leadership, and catalyze new climate pledges.

Counters 21st Century Challenges and Threats. The Budget prioritizes the need to counter the threat from China while also deterring destabilizing behavior by Russia. Leveraging the

Pacific Deterrence Initiative and working together with allies and partners in the Indo-Pacific region and the North Atlantic Treaty Organization, DOD would ensure that the United States builds the concepts, capabilities, and posture necessary to meet these challenges. To ensure the United States plays a lead role in defending democracy, freedom, and the rule of law, the Budget also includes a significant increase in resources to: strengthen and defend democracies throughout the world; advance human rights; fight corruption; and counter authoritarianism. In addition, to support agencies as they modernize, strengthen, and secure antiquated information systems and bolster Federal cybersecurity, the Budget provides $500 million for the Technology Modernization Fund, an additional $110 million for the Cybersecurity and Infrastructure Security Agency, and $750 million in additional investments tailored to respond to lessons learned from the SolarWinds incident.

Strengthens the Nation's Immigration and Asylum Systems. The Budget proposes resources to implement a fair, orderly, and humane immigration system. This includes resources necessary to fulfill the President's commitment to rebuild the Nation's badly damaged refugee admissions program and support up to 125,000 admissions in 2022. In addition, the Budget provides over $10 billion in humanitarian assistance to support vulnerable people abroad, including refugees and conflict victims. The Budget also includes resources to address the naturalization and asylum backlogs, support non-profit legal service providers to help vulnerable populations, and fund non-profit case management programs. The Budget would also revitalize U.S. leadership in Central America as part of a comprehensive strategy to address the root causes of irregular migration from Central America to the United States, providing $861 million in assistance to the region. These specific investments complement the President's legislative efforts to provide a path to citizenship for undocumented immigrants and implement an immigration system that welcomes all communities

Upholds the Nation's Sacred Obligation to America's Veterans. Building on significant investments included in the American Rescue Plan, the Budget proposes $97.5 billion to improve access to VA healthcare, an increase of $3.3 billion above the 2022 enacted advance appropriations level, including increases in funding for women's health, mental health, suicide prevention, and veterans' homeless programs. The Budget also proposes $882 million for medical and prosthetic research—including the largest increase in recent history—to advance VA's understanding of traumatic brain injury, the effects of toxic exposure on long-term health outcomes, and the needs of disabled veterans. In addition, the Budget includes $394 million to ensure veterans and their families have access to world-class memorial benefits.

THE PRESIDENT'S HEALTHCARE AGENDA TO LOWER COSTS AND EXPAND AND IMPROVE COVERAGE

The Patient Protection and Affordable Care Act (ACA) made historic progress in expanding and improving health coverage and lowering health costs. The American Rescue Plan built on that progress with the most substantial improvement in healthcare affordability since 2010. For people who obtain coverage through the ACA marketplaces, the American Rescue Plan increased premium tax credits—and extended them to families with incomes above 400 percent of the Federal poverty level—for two years. These improvements are lowering premiums for more than nine million current enrollees by an average of $50 per person per month, and would enable millions of uninsured people to gain coverage.

The American Rescue Plan was only a first step to lowering costs and expanding coverage. Building on that progress, the American Jobs Plan invests $400 billion in strengthening home- and community-based services for older people and people with disabilities and strengthening the workforce that provides this vital care. The American Families Plan makes permanent the American Rescue Plan's expansion of premium tax credits and makes a historic investment to improve maternal health and mortality.

Beyond these steps, the President also calls on the Congress to take action this year to reduce prescription drug costs and to further expand and improve health coverage. The President's healthcare agenda in these areas includes the following additional policies:

Lowering the Costs of Prescription Drugs. The President supports reforms that would bring down drug prices by letting Medicare negotiate payment for certain high-cost drugs and requiring manufacturers to pay rebates when drug prices rise faster than inflation. These reforms would lower drug costs and save money for Medicare beneficiaries and people with job-based insurance. The reforms could also yield over half a trillion in Federal savings over 10 years, which could help pay for coverage expansions and improvements.

Improving Medicare, Medicaid, and ACA Coverage. Medicare, Medicaid, and the ACA marketplaces provide critical coverage to tens of millions of Americans, but should be strengthened through measures like improving access to dental, hearing, and vision coverage in Medicare, making it easier for eligible people to get and stay covered in Medicaid, and reducing deductibles for marketplace plans. The President also supports eliminating Medicaid funding caps for Puerto Rico and other Territories while aligning their matching rate with States (and moving toward parity for other critical Federal programs including Supplemental Security Income and the Supplemental Nutrition Assistance Program). Further, evidence shows that we can reform Medicare payments to insurers and certain providers to reduce overpayments and strengthen incentives to deliver value-based care, extending the life of the Medicare Trust Fund, lowering premiums for beneficiaries, and reducing Federal costs.

Creating Additional Public Coverage Options. The President supports providing Americans with additional, lower-cost coverage choices by: creating a public option that would be available through the ACA marketplaces; and giving people age 60 and older the option to enroll in the Medicare program with the same premiums and benefits as current beneficiaries, but with financing separate from the Medicare Trust Fund. In States that have not expanded Medicaid, the President has proposed extending coverage to millions of people by providing premium-free, Medicaid-like coverage through a Federal public option, paired with financial incentives to ensure States maintain their existing expansions.

Healthcare is a right, not a privilege. Families need the financial security and peace of mind that comes with quality, affordable health coverage. In collaboration with the Congress, the President's healthcare agenda would achieve this promise.

THE IMPACT OF THE PRESIDENT'S POLICIES ON THE NATION'S ECONOMIC AND BUDGET OUTLOOK

The Budget makes the investments needed for economic growth and shared prosperity, while also putting the Nation on a sound fiscal course.

Generating Economic Growth and Shared Prosperity

The Budget makes historic investments that would increase economic prosperity over the coming decade and beyond by increasing American productivity and the number of good-paying American jobs. The President's investments are targeted to the everyday Americans who drive the economy forward. The Budget reflects the basic understanding that workers and families all over the Nation are the engines of America's prosperity and including more people in that prosperity is how the Nation thrives.

The Budget's investments in infrastructure, research, and other areas would make American businesses and workers more productive, and more productive businesses would increase hiring and pay higher wages. Rebuilding the Nation's infrastructure would bridge income and racial gaps in transportation and housing opportunities, create good union jobs, and enable businesses to deliver goods and services more affordably and operate anywhere, including in rural areas that currently lack broadband. Investments in R&D would ensure that the technologies of the future would be created in America by American businesses with American workers. Investments in manufacturing supply chains would make it more profitable to produce critical goods here at home and put more Americans to work in good jobs. In addition, investments to reverse climate change and develop climate resilience would drive technology growth, create millions of well-paying jobs with a free and fair choice to join a union, and mitigate the risk of electricity blackouts and other environmental disasters that disrupt work and cause enormous economic damage.

In addition to raising workers' wages, the Budget makes critical investments that would increase the total number of American jobs and ensure more of them are good-quality union jobs. A generational investment in America's caregiving infrastructure would enable millions of Americans—disproportionately women—to succeed in the workforce and receive the better pay they deserve as they raise children or care for ailing parents. Long overdue paid family and medical leave would ensure that no American worker is one pregnancy or illness away from losing their paycheck and reduce racial disparities in paid leave. Expanding the Earned Income Tax Credit would make it possible for more people to join and remain in the workforce. Health investments—from providing clean water to upgrading the public health system to expanding health insurance tax credits so that millions of people gain coverage and access to care—would lower mortality and disability and enable more Americans to work long healthy fulfilling careers.

The Budget also makes historic investments in children that would improve their health and well-being in the near term while contributing to economic growth and shared prosperity in the long term. Universal preschool, child nutrition expansions, and tax cuts that lift millions of families with children out of poverty would ensure that all children—not only those from privileged backgrounds or advantaged communities—are set up for success in school and beyond. Historic investments in Title I school funding would help millions of children in low-income families to compete through high school and beyond. Free community college and Pell Grants, along with investments in registered apprenticeships, other labor-management training programs, and other workforce training investments in the American Jobs Plan, would give students the support to build skills directly applicable to good-paying jobs. A large and growing body of research shows that these and similar investments not only yield immediate benefits for children and their families but also improve children's health and well-being and increase their earnings when they reach adulthood, strengthening America's future economy.

Overall, the Budget represents a comprehensive strategy to build an economy that works for everyone, not only the wealthy and well-connected. These investments would pay dividends for decades to come and would help build a high-skilled workforce, spur faster growth, and create more jobs, higher wages, more security, less poverty, less racial inequity, and broader prosperity.

Putting the Nation on a Fiscally Responsible Path

The Budget charts a fiscally responsible path for delivering a stronger, more prosperous economy. Under the Budget's proposals, the cost of Federal debt payments would remain well below historical levels throughout the coming decade. In response to the Nation's longer-term fiscal challenges, the Budget's proposals would reduce the deficit in later years.

Over the past several decades, interest rates have fallen, even as debt has risen. This has been a widespread, persistent, and global phenomenon, and it has meant that the burden associated with debt has decreased. Given these structural dynamics, the level of interest payments, rather than the size of the debt, is the most relevant benchmark for whether debt is burdening the economy.

Real interest—the Federal Government's annual interest payments after adjusting for inflation—directly measures the economic cost of the debt: the real resources that are going toward paying off old debt, instead of investing in the future.

Real interest has averaged about one percent of the economy since 1980 and was about two percent in the 1990s. Since then, the effective real interest rate on Federal debt has fallen 10-fold, from over 4 percent to 0.4 percent.

As a result, real interest has fallen. Strikingly, in 2021, real interest costs are expected to be negative, due to negative real interest rates. The Budget's economic forecast anticipates that real interest rates would likely rise over the coming decade, using projections in line with private forecasters. Nonetheless, under the President's policies, including the American Jobs Plan and the American Families Plan, real interest would remain at or below 0.5 percent of the economy throughout the next 10 years, well below the historical average.

In the current economic environment, the Federal Government has the fiscal space to make critical investments to expand the productive capacity of the economy, while also keeping real interest cost burdens low by historical standards. In fact, failing to make investments now that support growth and shared prosperity would leave future generations worse off.

Over the long term, the United States does face fiscal challenges, driven principally by underlying demographic pressures on health and retirement programs and inadequate revenue levels. There is also uncertainty about the interest rate outlook. The Budget's proposals prudently address these future challenges by making sure that new proposals are not only fully offset, but reduce deficits in the long run and improve the long-term fiscal outlook.

The Budget achieves this through reforms to the tax system. The Budget provides reforms to the corporate tax code to incentivize job creation and investment in the United States, stop unfair and wasteful profit shifting to tax havens, ensure that large corporations are paying their fair share, and stop a race-to-the-bottom in corporate tax rates around the world. The Budget also proposes to revitalize tax enforcement to ensure that high-income Americans pay the tax they owe under the law—ending the unfair system of enforcement that collects almost all taxes due on wages, while regularly collecting a smaller share of business and capital income. The plan would eliminate long-standing loopholes, including lower taxes on capital gains and dividends for the wealthy, which reward wealth over work.

Over time, the savings from these reforms would exceed the cost of the investments, and by large and growing amounts. The American Jobs Plan and American Families Plan together are paid for over 15 years. The full set of proposals in the Budget reduce the annual deficit by the end of the 10-year budget window and every year thereafter. In the second decade, the Budget's proposals reduce deficits by over $2 trillion.

A Budget that added to long-term deficits would worsen fiscal health, while a Budget that reduced deficits today by underinvesting in the American people would result in slower, more stratified growth that would cause more damage than one that invests appropriately. The Budget responsibly balances these needs and risks by charting an economically and fiscally sound course for the near term and the long term.

DELIVERING RESULTS FOR ALL AMERICANS THROUGH AN EQUITABLE, EFFECTIVE, AND ACCOUNTABLE GOVERNMENT

In order to build back better and meet the full range of challenges and opportunities before us, the Nation needs an equitable, effective, and accountable Government that delivers results for all Americans. The President is committed to ensuring the Government works for all Americans—and the Budget makes crucial progress toward achieving that goal. The Budget ensures Federal agencies are sufficiently resourced and effectively equipped to carry out their missions. The Budget would help bolster the Administration's efforts to: center equity across the Federal Government; empower, rebuild, and protect the Federal workforce; restore public trust in the Federal Government; deliver services effectively and efficiently; enhance Federal information technology (IT) and cybersecurity; advance America's clean energy future; and help ensure the future is made in America by all of America's workers. Taken together, these actions will support the President's Management Agenda as it takes shape in the coming months.

Centering Equity in Management and Policymaking Processes

The Administration is committed to delivering on the President's promise to advance equity across the entire Federal Government, including for people of color and other underserved communities that have been historically denied fair, just, and equitable treatment.

On January 26, 2021, the President said, "we need to make the issue of racial equity not just an issue for any one department of [G]overnment; it has to be the business of the whole of [G]overnment. That's why I issued, among the first days, my whole-of-[G]overnment [E]xecutive [O]rder that will, for the first time, advance equity for all throughout our [F]ederal policies and institutions." Through this action, the President has made embedding equity in Government decision-making a mandate for the leadership and staff of every department and agency. At the President's direction, agencies are working to recognize and redress inequities in their systems, policies, programs, and processes. Agencies are directed to review policies and activities to assess whether underserved communities and their members face systemic barriers in accessing benefits and opportunities available pursuant to those policies and programs. The President also issued an Executive Order creating the Gender Policy Council and laying out a whole-of-Government approach to ensure that all policies and programs promote gender equity and advance rights and opportunity for women and girls. As discussed in the previous chapter, the Budget makes wide-ranging investments in improving the delivery of Government programs for all Americans, including funding for critical work to redress long-standing inequities in health, education, housing, and other areas.

Empowering, Rebuilding, and Protecting the Federal Workforce

The Administration is committed to respecting and partnering with career civil servants who form the backbone of the Federal Government. That is why during his first month in office, the President restored collective bargaining rights and worker protections for Federal employees. The President eliminated Schedule F, which threatened the foundations of the civil service, and made clear that the Administration will protect scientists and other career civil servants from political interference. The President also signed an Executive Order to ensure that the Federal Government interprets Title VII of the Civil Rights Act of 1964 as prohibiting workplace discrimination on the basis of sexual orientation and gender identity.

The Budget builds on these efforts to empower and protect the Federal workforce by:

Supporting Career Civil Servants as the Backbone of the Federal Workforce. To help departments and agencies recruit and retain a diverse and inclusive Federal workforce, the Budget ensures more Federal employees are eligible for a $15 per hour wage, and provides funding for a pay increase averaging 2.7 percent across the Federal civilian workforce, in parity with the military pay increase. The President also took steps on his first day in office to protect the health and safety of Federal employees and contractors during the COVID-19 pandemic, including enforcing the Centers for Disease Control and Prevention's science-based guidelines and directing agencies to finalize and implement workplace health and safety plans. The President also made clear that he encourages union organizing and collective bargaining by revoking Executive Orders 13836, 13837, and 13839 that made it harder for Federal workers to unionize and bargain. The President's Executive Order on Protecting the Federal Workforce also directs agencies to bargain over additional subjects of bargaining, so that workers have a greater voice in their working conditions.

Achieving Better Hiring Outcomes. The Budget supports agency efforts to expand and enhance recruitment and hiring of top talent, and to deploy more effective qualifying assessments to improve hiring outcomes. Specifically, agencies would be required to revitalize their internship programs to begin to reverse the decline in the percentage of the workforce under 30, create and fund agency talent teams, and contribute funding to a new office that would support centralized Government-wide hiring actions that improve hiring outcomes for critical positions. Further, the President's Memorandum on

Revitalizing America's Foreign Policy and National Security Workforce, Institutions, and Partnerships ordered a series of actions agencies must take to ensure that the national security workforce reflects and draws on the richness and diversity of the Nation it represents.

Modernizing the Personnel Vetting System. The Administration is leading efforts to reform how the Executive Branch conducts background checks for its workforce through the Security Clearance, Suitability, and Credentialing Performance Accountability Council (PAC). The PAC is spearheading several transformative reforms through the Trusted Workforce 2.0 initiative that will introduce continuous vetting, reduce the time required to conduct background checks for new hires, and improve the mobility of the workforce, all while ensuring the Nation's security.

Promoting Public Trust in the Federal Government

As the President has said, "[w]e have to prove to the American people that their [G]overnment can deliver for them..." The Administration is making important progress in promoting trust in Government, and the Budget advances these efforts.

Recommitting to Good Government. As part of the Administration's commitment to good government, Federal agencies are working with external stakeholders and their own workforces to develop goals and track progress to improve the delivery of Government services in key priority areas. As the President's Management Agenda takes shape and agency goals are established and pursued, the public will be able to follow progress on Performance.gov, which will be updated quarterly. By being clear about the Administration's goals, showing the public plans to get there, and being transparent about results, the Administration will continue building trust with the American public.

Ensuring Effective Implementation of COVID-19 Pandemic Relief Funds and Stewardship of Taxpayer Resources. The Administration will administer COVID-19

pandemic relief funding—including funding provided through the American Rescue Plan Act of 2021 (the American Rescue Plan)—with maximum accountability and transparency and a focus on achieving results. This requires designing programs and service delivery models that achieve equitable results while promoting transparency and supporting long-term outcomes that benefit the American people. These goals can be achieved while minimizing burden to agencies and recipients through sound financial management, a focus on program integrity, and accurate and timely reporting on data about the use of taxpayer funds.

Fostering Scientific Integrity and Evidence-Based Decision-Making. The President has made clear that it is the policy of this Administration to make decisions guided by the best available science and data. On January 27, 2021, when signing a Presidential Memorandum charging agencies to advance scientific integrity and evidence-based policymaking, the President committed that his Administration would "protect our world-class scientists from political interference and ensure they can think, research, and speak freely and directly to me, the Vice President, and the American people." Evidence-based policy-making and program evaluation are critical in addressing systemic inequities and injustices and maintaining the public's trust. The Administration's commitment to evidence-based policy-making and program evaluation is reflected in the prioritization and design of the Budget's historic investments in addressing climate change, environmental justice, health security, and pandemic preparedness and will be equally central to implementing these initiatives. Agencies' Learning Agendas and Annual Evaluation Plans should reflect their plans to build evidence in these and other priority areas.

Delivering Government Services Effectively and Efficiently

Improving Customer Experience. The Federal Government administers a wide array of programs on behalf of the American people, but implementation efforts often fail to adopt a human, customer-focused mindset—preventing these programs from reaching all those they are intended to benefit and serve. The Administration is implementing a comprehensive approach to improving the access, equity, and overall delivery of Federal services, which includes improving customer experience management. The Budget supports the Nation's highest impact service providers across a variety of agencies to deliver on their annual Customer Experience Action Plans. This includes, for example: increasing the use of remote inspection capabilities to enable families to send the Federal Emergency Management Agency digital video and images of disaster property damage for verification and validation; making it possible for individuals to request a call back, rather than waiting on the phone, for more Internal Revenue Service functions; collecting customer feedback on interactions with the Transportation Security Administration from passengers that experience secondary screening; and adapting the design of new "journey to discharge" approaches at the Veterans Health Administration for patient information to reduce preventable adverse events within three weeks of discharge.

Delivering Better Services through Design and Technology. Too often, outdated tools, systems, and practices make interacting with the Federal Government cumbersome and frustrating. The COVID-19 pandemic laid bare and exacerbated the Government's technology and service delivery challenges in a time of immediate need. Recognizing this, the Administration requested and received $200 million through the American Rescue Plan for the United States Digital Service (USDS) for a multiyear investment in the USDS mission to use design and technology to deliver better services to the American people. USDS quickly deployed teams of seasoned operational engineers, service designers, product managers, and procurement experts to bring best practices and new approaches to these technology challenges, ensure access and equity are integrated into products and processes, and help agencies modernize their systems for long-term stability. USDS is integrally engaged on American Rescue Plan projects and Administration priorities for

COVID-19 pandemic vaccines and testing, economic rescue and recovery, environmental justice, and immigration reform.

Enhancing Federal IT and Cybersecurity

Modernizing Federal IT Systems. In a world of constantly evolving technology and expanding cybersecurity threats, the Administration recognizes the critical need for additional investment in enhancing Federal IT to improve service delivery to the American public. To support agencies as they modernize, strengthen, and secure outdated information systems, the Budget includes $500 million for the Technology Modernization Fund (TMF). This builds on the substantial down-payment provided by the Congress in the American Rescue Plan to address urgent IT modernization challenges, bolster cybersecurity defenses, and improve the delivery of COVID-19 pandemic relief. The TMF would continue to serve as the predominant vehicle for delivering improvements to public-facing digital services, enhancements to cross-government collaboration, and modern technology designed with security and privacy in mind.

Bolstering Federal Cybersecurity. Cybersecurity will continue to be a key focus in protecting this Nation's security, and recent, significant cybersecurity incidents highlight the long-standing need to modernize Federal IT systems and augment cybersecurity capabilities. The Budget contains $9.8 billion in cybersecurity funding to secure Federal civilian networks, protect the Nation's infrastructure, and support efforts to share information, standards, and best practices with critical infrastructure partners and American businesses. This funding includes $110 million for the Cybersecurity and Infrastructure Security Agency (CISA) and $750 million to agencies affected by recent, significant cyber incidents to address exigent gaps in security capability. These resources would better enable Federal agencies to protect technology and safeguard citizen's sensitive information from the threats posed by cyber criminals and adversaries. Agencies will continue to improve

cybersecurity practices, implement supply chain risk management programs, develop coordinated vulnerability disclosure programs, and improve cyber threat intelligence analysis. The Budget also provides $15 million to support the Office of the National Cyber Director established in the William M. (Mac) Thornberry National Defense Authorization Act for Fiscal Year 2021.

Improving the Federal IT Workforce. To support the Federal IT and cybersecurity portfolio, the Budget proposes to identify and address critical skills gaps across the IT and cybersecurity workforce. The Budget invests in innovative programs that improve the Government's ability to recruit, retain, and train a workforce that can build, maintain, and secure Federal information and information systems. The Administration is focused on continuing the use of reskilling and upskilling training programs to address critical knowledge skills gaps by reinvesting in existing employees. Moreover, the American Rescue Plan includes resources for USDS and CISA to hire information technology and cybersecurity experts.

Ensuring the Future Is Made in All of America by All of America's Workers

Supporting America's Workers and America's Clean Energy Future through Federal Contracting. The Administration will leverage over $600 billion in annual Federal contracting and other Federal assistance—nearly $260 billion of which is spent on manufactured goods each year—to provide good-quality jobs to American workers in manufacturing by strengthening domestic sourcing requirements. This includes the establishment of a Made in America Office within the Office of Management and Budget that works with the Office of Federal Procurement Policy to ensure taxpayer dollars support American manufacturing. Agencies will also leverage their vast buying power to advance racial equity using procurement strategies to expand and strengthen the Government's contracting base, especially in underserved communities, and drive forward America's clean energy future. For example, the Budget invests $600 million to assist agencies in transitioning to clean and zero-emission vehicles for Government fleets and associated infrastructure, leading the way for a cleaner transportation network across America. The President also issued an Executive Order on April 27, 2021 requiring Federal contractors pay their employees—hundreds of thousands of workers who are working on Federal contracts—a minimum wage of at least $15 per hour. These workers are critical to the functioning of the Federal Government: from cleaning professionals and maintenance workers who ensure Federal employees have safe and clean places to work; to nursing assistants who care for the Nation's veterans; to cafeteria and other food service workers who ensure military members have healthy and nutritious food to eat; to laborers who build and repair Federal infrastructure.

Providing for a Modern and Diverse Federal Acquisition System. The Federal Government's ability to effectively meet its many missions requires support from a diverse and resilient contractor base of small, medium, and large entities that consistently produce high-quality products and services with strong customer satisfaction. The purchasing power of the Federal Government has the potential to have a transformative impact on women-, veteran-, and minority-owned small businesses and create generational wealth for business owners from traditionally underserved communities. To meet this dual challenge, the Administration will pursue agile, innovative, outcome-based, and equity-focused, acquisition processes. This will include a dedicated effort to eliminate barriers that small businesses in underserved communities face when competing for contracts. In addition, the Administration will provide the acquisition workforce with supplier and market intelligence data at the point of need, so they can work productively with contractors from across the Nation to achieve more for each taxpayer dollar by, among other things, promoting buying as an organized entity and using strategic business practices. Additional emphasis will be placed on partnering with entities that leverage domestic supply chains, and sources that apply climate-friendly and sustainable practices.

Summary Tables

Table S–1. Budget Totals
(In billions of dollars and as a percent of GDP)

	2020	2021	2022	2023	2024	2025	2026	2027	2028	2029	2030	2031	Totals 2022-2026	Totals 2022-2031
Budget totals in billions of dollars:														
Receipts	3,421	3,581	4,174	4,641	4,828	5,038	5,332	5,632	5,888	6,119	6,370	6,643	24,013	54,665
Outlays	6,550	7,249	6,011	6,013	6,187	6,508	6,746	6,935	7,312	7,425	7,847	8,211	31,465	69,196
Deficit[1]	3,129	3,669	1,837	1,372	1,359	1,470	1,414	1,303	1,424	1,307	1,477	1,568	7,452	14,531
Debt held by the public	21,017	24,167	26,265	27,683	29,062	30,539	31,958	33,266	34,691	35,996	37,481	39,059		
Debt held by the public net of financial assets	18,024	21,684	23,520	24,892	26,250	27,720	29,134	30,437	31,860	33,167	34,643	36,216		
Gross domestic product (GDP)	21,000	22,030	23,500	24,563	25,537	26,516	27,533	28,590	29,697	30,867	32,094	33,391		
Budget totals as a percent of GDP:														
Receipts	16.3%	16.3%	17.8%	18.9%	18.9%	19.0%	19.4%	19.7%	19.8%	19.8%	19.8%	19.9%	18.8%	19.3%
Outlays	31.2%	32.9%	25.6%	24.5%	24.2%	24.5%	24.5%	24.3%	24.6%	24.1%	24.4%	24.6%	24.7%	24.5%
Deficit	14.9%	16.7%	7.8%	5.6%	5.3%	5.5%	5.1%	4.6%	4.8%	4.2%	4.6%	4.7%	5.9%	5.2%
Debt held by the public	100.1%	109.7%	111.8%	112.7%	113.8%	115.2%	116.1%	116.4%	116.8%	116.6%	116.8%	117.0%		
Debt held by the public net of financial assets	85.8%	98.4%	100.1%	101.3%	102.8%	104.5%	105.8%	106.5%	107.3%	107.5%	107.9%	108.5%		
Memorandum, real net interest:														
Real net interest in billions of dollars	134	–53	–139	–189	–186	–136	–86	–36	9	50	108	164	–737	–442
Real net interest as a percent of GDP	0.6%	–0.2%	–0.6%	–0.8%	–0.7%	–0.5%	–0.3%	–0.1%	*	0.2%	0.3%	0.5%	–0.6%	–0.2%

*0.05 percent of GDP or less.

[1] The estimated deficit for 2021 is based on partial year actual data and generally incorporates actuals through March.

Table S–2. Effect of Budget Proposals on Projected Deficits

(Deficit increases (+) or decreases (–) in billions of dollars)

	2020	2021	2022	2023	2024	2025	2026	2027	2028	2029	2030	2031	Totals 2022–2026	Totals 2022–2031
Projected deficits in the baseline	3,129	3,670	1,719	1,148	1,068	1,176	1,115	1,134	1,348	1,291	1,517	1,660	6,226	13,176
Percent of GDP	14.9%	16.7%	7.3%	4.7%	4.2%	4.4%	4.0%	4.0%	4.5%	4.2%	4.7%	5.0%		
Proposals in the 2022 Budget:														
Enact the American Jobs Plan	....	....	84	92	141	152	177	110	28	–35	–87	–133	645	529
Enact the American Families Plan	....	–1	16	79	88	78	53	–9	–17	–9	–5	–2	312	270
Restore non-defense discretionary spending and provide robust funding for national defense[1]	....	....	19	53	59	56	54	48	40	32	23	10	241	393
Debt service and other interest effects	....	–*	*	*	3	9	15	22	25	27	30	31	27	163
Total proposals in the 2022 Budget	....	–1	118	224	291	294	299	170	76	15	–40	–93	1,226	1,355
Resulting deficits in the 2022 Budget	3,129	3,669	1,837	1,372	1,359	1,470	1,414	1,303	1,424	1,307	1,477	1,568	7,452	14,531
Percent of GDP	14.9%	16.7%	7.8%	5.6%	5.3%	5.5%	5.1%	4.6%	4.8%	4.2%	4.6%	4.7%		

	2032	2033	2034	2035	2036	2037	2038	2039	2040	2041	Cumulative Totals 2022–2036	Cumulative Totals 2022–2041
Memorandum:												
Enact the American Jobs Plan and the American Families Plan, second decade effect	–165	–217	–228	–238	–248	–260	–272	–285	–299	–313	–297	–1,726
Total proposals in the 2022 Budget, second decade effect	–126	–183	–198	–213	–229	–246	–264	–282	–302	–323	–406	–1,012

*$500 million or less

[1] Includes mandatory effects of discretionary policy and other conforming technical adjustments

Table S-3. Baseline by Category [1]

(In billions of dollars)

	2020	2021	2022	2023	2024	2025	2026	2027	2028	2029	2030	2031	Totals 2022-2026	Totals 2022-2031
Outlays:														
Discretionary programs:														
Defense	714	735	754	756	778	796	811	828	846	865	884	903	3,895	8,221
Non-defense	913	960	913	874	842	849	851	862	880	896	913	931	4,329	8,810
Subtotal, discretionary programs	1,627	1,696	1,667	1,630	1,621	1,645	1,661	1,689	1,726	1,760	1,797	1,834	8,224	17,031
Mandatory programs:														
Social Security	1,090	1,135	1,196	1,261	1,333	1,410	1,493	1,580	1,673	1,769	1,868	1,969	6,694	15,553
Medicare	769	709	767	842	842	948	1,016	1,087	1,229	1,181	1,328	1,415	4,414	10,654
Medicaid	458	521	518	529	563	592	621	654	698	741	783	828	2,823	6,528
Other mandatory programs	2,260	2,886	1,255	870	795	784	806	813	877	846	900	938	4,510	8,885
Subtotal, mandatory programs	4,578	5,251	3,735	3,503	3,533	3,735	3,935	4,135	4,478	4,537	4,879	5,149	18,441	41,620
Net interest	345	303	305	319	365	436	509	581	649	717	798	883	1,935	5,563
Total outlays	6,550	7,249	5,707	5,453	5,519	5,816	6,106	6,405	6,854	7,015	7,475	7,866	28,600	64,215
Receipts:														
Individual income taxes	1,609	1,704	2,005	2,174	2,210	2,347	2,646	2,852	2,986	3,128	3,275	3,431	11,382	27,053
Corporation income taxes	212	268	266	367	412	432	425	424	433	432	433	438	1,902	4,062
Social insurance and retirement receipts:														
Social Security payroll taxes	965	944	1,032	1,068	1,113	1,153	1,202	1,247	1,305	1,355	1,410	1,467	5,568	12,352
Medicare payroll taxes	292	287	314	326	341	353	368	383	402	418	437	456	1,703	3,799
Unemployment insurance	43	55	59	61	60	57	55	55	57	57	58	56	294	577
Other retirement	10	10	11	12	12	13	13	14	15	16	17	17	62	140
Excise taxes	87	74	82	85	90	90	91	92	92	94	97	97	439	910
Estate and gift taxes	18	18	21	22	24	25	25	38	39	41	43	46	116	323
Customs duties	69	85	57	45	45	47	48	49	51	53	55	57	242	506
Deposits of earnings, Federal Reserve System	82	97	102	103	99	77	68	65	71	75	75	79	448	814
Other miscellaneous receipts	36	37	39	40	44	46	49	52	55	57	59	60	218	501
Total receipts	3,421	3,580	3,988	4,304	4,451	4,640	4,991	5,272	5,506	5,724	5,958	6,205	22,374	51,038
Deficit	3,129	3,670	1,719	1,148	1,068	1,176	1,115	1,134	1,348	1,291	1,517	1,660	6,226	13,176
Net interest	345	303	305	319	365	436	509	581	649	717	798	883	1,935	5,563
Primary deficit	2,784	3,367	1,414	829	703	739	606	553	699	574	718	778	4,291	7,613
On-budget deficit	3,142	3,597	1,670	1,074	969	1,041	955	938	1,122	1,021	1,205	1,307	5,710	11,303
Off-budget deficit/surplus (−)	−13	73	48	74	99	135	160	195	226	270	312	354	516	1,873

[1] Baseline estimates are on the basis of the economic assumptions shown in Table S-9, which incorporate the effects of the Administration's fiscal policies.

Table S–4. Proposed Budget by Category

(In billions of dollars)

	2020	2021	2022	2023	2024	2025	2026	2027	2028	2029	2030	2031	Totals 2022–2026	Totals 2022–2031
Outlays:														
Discretionary programs:														
Defense	714	735	756	756	775	791	804	816	826	835	843	851	3,881	8,052
Non-defense	913	960	932	930	909	914	917	927	947	964	984	1,002	4,601	9,426
Subtotal, discretionary programs	1,627	1,696	1,688	1,685	1,683	1,704	1,721	1,743	1,773	1,799	1,827	1,854	8,482	17,478
Mandatory programs:														
Social Security	1,090	1,135	1,196	1,261	1,333	1,410	1,492	1,579	1,672	1,767	1,866	1,966	6,691	15,542
Medicare	769	709	766	841	840	947	1,014	1,085	1,227	1,178	1,325	1,412	4,407	10,633
Medicaid	458	521	571	582	616	645	674	698	734	768	801	837	3,088	6,926
Other mandatory programs	2,260	2,886	1,486	1,324	1,347	1,357	1,321	1,227	1,232	1,168	1,200	1,228	6,835	12,891
Subtotal, mandatory programs	4,578	5,251	4,018	4,008	4,136	4,358	4,501	4,589	4,865	4,882	5,191	5,444	21,021	45,992
Net interest	345	303	305	320	368	445	524	603	674	744	829	914	1,962	5,726
Total outlays	6,550	7,249	6,011	6,013	6,187	6,508	6,746	6,935	7,312	7,425	7,847	8,211	31,465	69,196
Receipts:														
Individual income taxes	1,609	1,705	2,039	2,242	2,288	2,436	2,676	2,896	3,044	3,194	3,354	3,526	11,680	27,694
Corporation income taxes	212	268	371	577	649	673	664	666	679	678	681	693	2,933	6,330
Social insurance and retirement receipts:														
Social Security payroll taxes	965	944	1,033	1,072	1,118	1,159	1,207	1,252	1,311	1,361	1,417	1,474	5,587	12,403
Medicare payroll taxes	292	287	359	383	400	418	436	453	476	496	518	540	1,995	4,478
Unemployment insurance	43	55	59	61	60	57	55	55	57	56	58	56	293	576
Other retirement	10	10	11	12	12	13	13	14	15	16	17	17	62	140
Excise taxes	87	74	84	89	93	94	95	96	96	98	101	102	455	948
Estate and gift taxes	18	18	21	18	19	20	21	32	33	34	37	39	99	274
Customs duties	69	85	57	45	45	47	48	49	51	53	55	57	242	506
Deposits of earnings, Federal Reserve System	82	97	102	103	99	77	68	65	71	75	75	79	448	814
Other miscellaneous receipts	36	37	39	40	44	46	49	52	55	57	59	60	218	501
Total receipts	3,421	3,581	4,174	4,641	4,828	5,038	5,332	5,632	5,888	6,119	6,370	6,643	24,013	54,665
Deficit	3,129	3,669	1,837	1,372	1,359	1,470	1,414	1,303	1,424	1,307	1,477	1,568	7,452	14,531
Net interest	345	303	305	320	368	445	524	603	674	744	829	914	1,962	5,726
Primary deficit	2,784	3,366	1,532	1,052	991	1,025	890	701	749	562	649	654	5,490	8,805
On-budget deficit	3,142	3,595	1,789	1,301	1,264	1,341	1,260	1,115	1,205	1,045	1,174	1,223	6,956	12,718
Off-budget deficit/surplus (−)	−13	73	48	71	95	129	154	189	219	262	303	345	496	1,813

Table S–5. Proposed Budget by Category as a Percent of GDP
(As a percent of GDP)

	2020	2021	2022	2023	2024	2025	2026	2027	2028	2029	2030	2031	Averages 2022–2026	Averages 2022–2031
Outlays:														
Discretionary programs:														
Defense	3.4	3.3	3.2	3.1	3.0	3.0	2.9	2.9	2.8	2.7	2.6	2.5	3.0	2.9
Non-defense	4.3	4.4	4.0	3.8	3.6	3.4	3.3	3.2	3.2	3.1	3.1	3.0	3.6	3.4
Subtotal, discretionary programs	7.7	7.7	7.2	6.9	6.6	6.4	6.3	6.1	6.0	5.8	5.7	5.6	6.7	6.2
Mandatory programs:														
Social Security	5.2	5.2	5.1	5.1	5.2	5.3	5.4	5.5	5.6	5.7	5.8	5.9	5.2	5.5
Medicare	3.7	3.2	3.3	3.4	3.3	3.6	3.7	3.8	4.1	3.8	4.1	4.2	3.4	3.7
Medicaid	2.2	2.4	2.4	2.4	2.4	2.4	2.4	2.4	2.5	2.5	2.5	2.5	2.4	2.4
Other mandatory programs	10.8	13.1	6.3	5.4	5.3	5.1	4.8	4.3	4.1	3.8	3.7	3.7	5.4	4.7
Subtotal, mandatory programs	21.8	23.8	17.1	16.3	16.2	16.4	16.3	16.1	16.4	15.8	16.2	16.3	16.5	16.3
Net interest	1.6	1.4	1.3	1.3	1.4	1.7	1.9	2.1	2.3	2.4	2.6	2.7	1.5	2.0
Total outlays	31.2	32.9	25.6	24.5	24.2	24.5	24.5	24.3	24.6	24.1	24.4	24.6	24.7	24.5
Receipts:														
Individual income taxes	7.7	7.7	8.7	9.1	9.0	9.2	9.7	10.1	10.3	10.3	10.4	10.6	9.1	9.7
Corporation income taxes	1.0	1.2	1.6	2.3	2.5	2.5	2.4	2.3	2.3	2.2	2.1	2.1	2.3	2.2
Social insurance and retirement receipts:														
Social Security payroll taxes	4.6	4.3	4.4	4.4	4.4	4.4	4.4	4.4	4.4	4.4	4.4	4.4	4.4	4.4
Medicare payroll taxes	1.4	1.3	1.5	1.6	1.6	1.6	1.6	1.6	1.6	1.6	1.6	1.6	1.6	1.6
Unemployment insurance	0.2	0.2	0.3	0.2	0.2	0.2	0.2	0.2	0.2	0.2	0.2	0.2	0.2	0.2
Other retirement	*	*	*	*	*	*	*	*	*	0.1	0.1	0.1	*	*
Excise taxes	0.4	0.3	0.4	0.4	0.4	0.4	0.3	0.3	0.3	0.3	0.3	0.3	0.4	0.3
Estate and gift taxes	0.1	0.1	0.1	0.1	0.1	0.1	0.1	0.1	0.1	0.1	0.1	0.1	0.1	0.1
Customs duties	0.3	0.4	0.2	0.2	0.2	0.2	0.2	0.2	0.2	0.2	0.2	0.2	0.2	0.2
Deposits of earnings, Federal Reserve System	0.4	0.4	0.4	0.4	0.4	0.3	0.2	0.2	0.2	0.2	0.2	0.2	0.4	0.3
Other miscellaneous receipts	0.2	0.2	0.2	0.2	0.2	0.2	0.2	0.2	0.2	0.2	0.2	0.2	0.2	0.2
Total receipts	16.3	16.3	17.8	18.9	18.9	19.0	19.4	19.7	19.8	19.8	19.8	19.9	18.8	19.3
Deficit	14.9	16.7	7.8	5.6	5.3	5.5	5.1	4.6	4.8	4.2	4.6	4.7	5.9	5.2
Net interest	1.6	1.4	1.3	1.3	1.4	1.7	1.9	2.1	2.3	2.4	2.6	2.7	1.5	2.0
Primary deficit	13.3	15.3	6.5	4.3	3.9	3.9	3.2	2.5	2.5	1.8	2.0	2.0	4.4	3.3
On-budget deficit	15.0	16.3	7.6	5.3	5.0	5.1	4.6	3.9	4.1	3.4	3.7	3.7	5.5	4.6
Off-budget deficit/surplus (–)	–0.1	0.3	0.2	0.3	0.4	0.5	0.6	0.7	0.7	0.8	0.9	1.0	0.4	0.6

*0.05 percent of GDP or less.

Table S–6. Mandatory and Receipt Proposals

(Deficit increases (+) or decreases (–) in millions of dollars)

	2021	2022	2023	2024	2025	2026	2027	2028	2029	2030	2031	Totals 2022–2026	Totals 2022–2031
American Jobs Plan													
Build world-class transportation infrastructure:													
Transform our crumbling transportation infrastructure:													
Repair roads and bridges	......	5,124	13,385	17,416	19,650	21,626	16,958	7,895	4,523	3,310	2,408	77,201	112,295
Improve road safety for all users	......	414	1,427	2,279	3,062	3,872	3,404	1,696	1,174	948	746	11,054	19,022
Modernize public transit	......	1,830	4,225	6,085	7,090	9,395	11,765	13,400	10,855	7,455	4,540	28,625	76,640
Invest in reliable passenger and freight rail	......	1,600	2,850	4,880	7,497	10,209	11,209	11,725	10,453	7,898	5,279	27,036	73,600
Create good jobs electrifying vehicles:													
Spark widespread adoption of electric vehicles (EVs)	......	795	2,328	6,436	13,468	25,971	26,612	25,397	20,952	13,685	1,723	48,998	137,367
Invest in electric school buses	......	2,000	3,200	3,800	4,000	4,000	2,000	800	200	......	......	17,000	20,000
Improve ports, waterways, and airports:													
Invest in ports	......	......	5	95	310	680	1,090	1,360	1,230	855	375	1,090	6,000
Make our airports the best in the world	......	1,235	3,460	4,145	4,455	4,630	4,270	1,705	615	335	150	17,925	25,000
Improve coastal ports and inland waterways	......	3,488	1,411	1,406	1,060	635	......	......	......	......	......	8,000	8,000
Invest in the Federally owned Land Ports of Entry portfolio	......	15	80	250	515	750	765	475	150	......	......	1,610	3,000
Redress historic inequities and build the future of transportation infrastructure:													
Restore and reconnect thriving communities	......	236	964	1,860	2,684	3,575	4,104	3,868	3,219	2,244	1,242	9,319	23,996
Accelerate transformational projects	......	367	1,014	2,658	4,496	6,185	7,058	7,133	5,878	4,118	2,636	14,720	41,543
Total, transform our crumbling transportation infrastructure	......	17,104	34,349	51,310	68,287	91,528	89,235	75,454	59,249	40,848	19,099	262,578	546,463
Make our infrastructure more resilient:													
Safeguard critical infrastructure and services:													
Enhance electric grid resilience, including cyber	......	40	180	420	600	460	190	80	30	......	......	1,700	2,000
Urban Heat Stress:													
Map heat stress	......	30	30	30	30	30	30	30	30	30	30	150	300
Mitigate heat stress	......	120	192	228	240	240	120	48	12	......	......	1,020	1,200
Community health and hospital resilience:													
Increase resilience of hospitals and critical infrastructure	......	270	580	90	60	......	......	......	......	......	......	1,000	1,000
Fund health emergency preparedness	......	22	195	20	8	5	......	......	......	......	......	250	250
Build resilience against climate effects	......	68	145	22	15	......	......	......	......	......	......	250	250
Maximize the resilience of land and water resources to protect communities and the environment:													
Ecosystem resilience, green infrastructure, and conservation on Federal, Tribal and partner lands:													
Deploy green and conservation-based infrastructure	......	240	600	960	1,200	1,200	960	600	240	......	......	4,200	6,000
Invest in Tribal fuels management	......	40	100	140	170	200	160	100	60	30	......	650	1,000
Invest in natural resource restoration grants and partnerships	......	160	400	640	800	800	640	400	160	......	......	2,800	4,000
Improve coastal resilience	......	250	250	250	250	250	250	250	250	250	250	1,250	2,500

Table S–6.　Mandatory and Receipt Proposals—Continued

(Deficit increases (+) or decreases (−) in millions of dollars)

	2021	2022	2023	2024	2025	2026	2027	2028	2029	2030	2031	Totals 2022–2026	Totals 2022–2031
Increase the resilience of large landscape ecosystems	....	400	400	400	400	400	400	400	200	....	....	2,000	3,000
Increase western water resilience	....	300	500	500	500	500	200	....	....	....	....	2,300	2,500
Community resilience and equity:													
Support disadvantaged community investment in hazard mitigation projects, including incentives for building above existing codes and standards:													
Invest in disadvantaged communities through the Building Resilient Infrastructure in Communities grant program	....	....	....	....	40	300	380	480	460	200	120	340	1,980
Provide Community Development Block Grants for resilience	....	5	165	340	435	470	485	330	160	65	30	1,415	2,485
Invest in a National resilient communities challenge	....	....	21	91	197	320	433	487	420	284	146	629	2,399
Improve transportation infrastructure resilience (PROTECT grants)	....	75	262	425	613	825	800	475	438	378	295	2,200	4,586
Flood and drought resilience for vulnerable communities:													
Establish an affordability program for the National Flood Insurance Program	....	194	235	349	400	471	523	568	591	587	626	1,649	4,544
Invest in watershed protection and flood prevention	....	5	30	90	96	99	100	100	100	100	100	320	820
Invest in technology to increase drought resilience for agricultural producers	....	18	32	40	44	48	50	50	50	50	50	182	432
Support agriculture resource management and improve irrigation for Tribes and insular areas	....	50	80	100	100	100	50	20	....	....	....	430	500
Provide pre-development grants for resilient infrastructure	....	140	400	400	400	400	260	....	....	....	....	1,740	2,000
Provide community transition and relocation assistance	....	80	200	320	400	400	320	200	80	....	....	1,400	2,000
Support resilience tools to build back better:													
Hazard mapping:													
Update flood and hazard maps in disadvantaged communities	....	60	105	105	30	....	....	....	....	....	....	300	300
Expand ocean and coastal mapping	....	50	50	50	50	50	50	50	50	50	50	250	500
Improve digital high-resolution elevation collection mapping	....	40	50	40	40	30	....	....	....	....	....	200	200
Improve climate forecast capabilities and information products for the public and monitoring the impacts of climate change:													
Provide localized information to help communities respond to climate change	....	32	80	128	160	160	128	80	32	....	....	560	800
Improve local air and water quality monitoring/modeling	....	20	32	38	40	40	20	8	2	....	....	170	200
Develop decision support tools	....	50	50	50	50	50	50	50	50	50	50	250	500
Invest in resilience financing mechanisms	....	70	200	200	200	200	130	....	....	....	....	870	1,000
Total, make our infrastructure more resilient	....	2,829	5,564	6,466	7,568	8,048	6,729	4,806	3,415	2,074	1,747	30,475	49,246
Total, build world-class transportation infrastructure	....	19,933	39,913	57,776	75,855	99,576	95,964	80,260	62,664	42,922	20,846	293,053	595,709

Table S–6. Mandatory and Receipt Proposals—Continued

(Deficit increases (+) or decreases (−) in millions of dollars)

	2021	2022	2023	2024	2025	2026	2027	2028	2029	2030	2031	Totals 2022–2026	Totals 2022–2031
Rebuild clean drinking water infrastructure, a renewed electrical grid, and high-speed broadband to all Americans:													
Ensure clean, safe drinking water is a right in all communities:													
Replace 100 percent of the Nation's lead service lines	....	4,500	7,200	8,550	9,000	9,000	4,500	1,800	450	....	....	38,250	45,000
Invest in Rural Clean Water infrastructure	....	195	260	650	1,300	1,755	2,340	....	....	....	....	4,160	6,500
Tackle new contaminants, including polyfluoroalkyl substances (PFAS)	....	350	560	665	700	700	350	140	35	....	....	2,975	3,500
Upgrade and modernize America's drinking water, wastewater, and stormwater systems	....	5,600	8,960	10,640	11,200	11,200	5,600	2,240	560	....	....	47,600	56,000
Total, ensure clean, safe drinking water is a right in all communities	....	10,645	16,980	20,505	22,200	22,655	12,790	4,180	1,045	....	....	92,985	111,000
Digital infrastructure, adoption, and affordability	....	13,000	48,000	23,000	8,000	8,000	....	....	....	....	....	100,000	100,000
Reenergize America's power infrastructure:													
Invest in hydrogen, carbon capture, and sequestration capacity	....	380	990	1,700	2,400	2,430	800	450	100	50	....	7,900	9,300
Provide clean energy block grants for early action	....	1,500	3,500	4,500	5,000	3,500	1,500	500	....	....	....	18,000	20,000
Provide community solar and storage assistance	....	100	200	400	300	....	....	....	....	....	....	1,000	1,000
Remediate and redevelop brownfield sites	....	500	800	950	1,000	1,000	500	200	50	....	....	4,250	5,000
Mobilize the Civilian Climate Corps	....	1,000	2,000	2,000	2,000	2,000	1,000	....	....	....	....	9,000	10,000
Expand the Public Works Program at the Economic Development Administration	....	227	270	300	358	300	45	....	....	....	....	1,455	1,500
Expand rural Main Street revitalization grants	....	38	110	55	25	22	....	....	....	....	....	250	250
Provide Main Street grants to small communities	....	12	66	58	58	2	55	....	....	....	....	196	251
Provide support for biofuels	....	500	250	250	....	....	....	....	....	....	....	1,000	1,000
Support economic development in Appalachian communities	....	2	66	136	174	188	194	132	64	26	12	566	994
Expand the Environmental Justice Small Grants program	....	250	400	475	500	500	250	100	25	....	....	2,125	2,500
Invest in lead remediation and healthy homes	....	12	66	240	438	564	582	534	360	162	36	1,320	2,994
Provide grants to convert and retool manufacturing facilities	....	200	340	500	670	200	90	....	....	....	....	1,910	2,000
Provide grants to replace leaking natural gas distribution lines	....	150	430	580	620	180	40	....	....	....	....	1,960	2,000
Reclaim abandoned mines and wells	....	640	1,440	2,400	2,880	3,200	2,560	1,760	800	320	....	10,560	16,000
Accelerate clean energy support to rural co-ops	....	2,400	3,200	1,800	1,200	1,400	....	....	....	....	....	10,000	10,000
Employ electrical workers upgrading the grid	....	240	1,080	2,520	3,600	2,760	1,140	480	180	....	....	10,200	12,000
Increase adoption of net-zero agriculture technology	....	172	194	104	105	129	115	85	56	22	10	704	992
Total, reenergize America's power infrastructure	....	8,311	15,354	18,968	21,328	18,435	8,871	4,241	1,635	580	58	82,396	97,781
Total, rebuild clean drinking water infrastructure, a renewed electrical grid, and high-speed broadband to all Americans	....	31,956	80,334	62,473	51,528	49,090	21,661	8,421	2,680	580	58	275,381	308,781

Table S–6. Mandatory and Receipt Proposals—Continued

(Deficit increases (+) or decreases (–) in millions of dollars)

	2021	2022	2023	2024	2025	2026	2027	2028	2029	2030	2031	Totals 2022–2026	Totals 2022–2031
Build, preserve, and retrofit more than two million homes and commercial buildings; modernize our Nation's schools, community colleges, and early learning facilities; and upgrade veterans' hospitals and Federal buildings:													
Build, preserve, and retrofit more than two million homes and commercial buildings to address the affordable housing crisis:													
Capitalize a clean energy accelerator	......	27,000	......	......	......	......	......	......	......	......	......	27,000	27,000
Provide efficiency/electrification block grants	......	1,600	2,800	3,200	2,900	1,600	700	200	......	......	......	12,100	13,000
Expand weatherization	......	1,750	5,050	6,100	3,400	1,200	......	......	......	......	......	17,500	17,500
Retrofit Housing and Urban Development multifamily properties	......	55	80	90	100	100	45	20	10	......	......	425	500
Expand the Capital Magnet Fund	......	2,400	2,400	2,400	2,400	2,400	......	......	......	......	......	12,000	12,000
Increase the Housing Trust Fund	......	......	90	1,260	4,140	6,840	8,640	8,820	7,740	4,860	2,160	12,330	44,550
Support housing and community development in Indian Country	......	2	46	134	240	328	370	342	266	160	72	750	1,960
Provide project-based rental assistance	......	130	200	200	200	200	200	200	200	200	200	930	1,930
Invest in the public housing stock	......	1,200	12,000	14,000	7,200	4,400	800	400	......	......	......	38,800	40,000
Construct housing for the elderly	......	2	46	134	240	328	370	342	266	160	72	750	1,960
Stimulate additional rural housing grants, loans, and loan guarantees	......	460	485	485	350	220	......	......	......	......	......	2,000	2,000
Incentivize zoning reform	......	30	330	680	860	970	960	670	320	140	30	2,870	4,990
Invest in Home Online Performance-Based Energy-Efficiency (HOPE) for homes	......	800	1,400	1,800	2,000	2,000	1,200	600	200	......	......	8,000	10,000
Provide HOME grants	......	35	805	2,345	4,200	5,740	6,475	5,985	4,655	2,800	1,260	13,125	34,300
Total, build, preserve, and retrofit more than two million homes and commercial buildings to address the affordable housing crisis	......	35,464	25,732	32,828	28,230	26,326	19,760	17,579	13,657	8,320	3,794	148,580	211,690
Modernize our Nation's schools and early learning facilities:													
Invest in child care infrastructure	......	2,500	4,000	4,750	5,000	5,000	2,500	1,000	250	......	......	21,250	25,000
Invest in community college infrastructure	......	240	888	2,064	2,400	2,400	2,160	1,512	336	......	......	7,992	12,000
Invest in K–12 school infrastructure	......	1,000	3,700	8,600	10,000	10,000	9,000	6,300	1,400	......	......	33,300	50,000
Total, modernize our Nation's schools and early learning facilities	......	3,740	8,588	15,414	17,400	17,400	13,660	8,812	1,986	......	......	62,542	87,000
Upgrade Federal hospitals and buildings:													
Invest in the General Service Administration Federal Buildings portfolio	......	100	450	850	1,000	1,000	900	550	150	......	......	3,400	5,000
Establish and capitalize the Federal Capital Revolving Fund	......	966	2,264	1,132	133	–133	117	–150	67	–13	–90	4,362	4,293
Veterans Affairs facility maintenance and modernization to deliver 21st Century care:													
Recapitalize long-term facilities	......	622	511	470	4,222	3,894	3,724	1,319	116	64	58	9,719	15,000
Perform short-term upgrades to facilities	......	6	23	62	149	410	878	752	419	231	70	650	3,000
Total, upgrade Federal hospitals and buildings	......	1,694	3,248	2,514	5,504	5,171	5,619	2,471	752	282	38	18,131	27,293
Total, build, preserve, and retrofit more than two million homes and commercial buildings; modernize our Nation's schools, community colleges, and early learning facilities; and upgrade veterans' hospitals and Federal buildings	......	40,898	37,568	50,756	51,134	48,897	39,039	28,862	16,395	8,602	3,832	229,253	325,983

Table S–6. Mandatory and Receipt Proposals—Continued

(Deficit increases (+) or decreases (–) in millions of dollars)

	2021	2022	2023	2024	2025	2026	2027	2028	2029	2030	2031	Totals 2022–2026	Totals 2022–2031
Solidify the infrastructure of our care economy by creating jobs and raising wages and benefits for essential home care workers:													
Expand Medicaid home and community based services and strengthen the home care workforce	....	53,000	53,000	53,000	53,000	53,000	44,000	36,000	27,000	18,000	10,000	265,000	400,000
Total, solidify the infrastructure of our care economy by creating jobs and raising wages and benefits for essential home care workers	....	53,000	53,000	53,000	53,000	53,000	44,000	36,000	27,000	18,000	10,000	265,000	400,000
Invest in research and development (R&D), revitalize manufacturing and small businesses, and train Americans for the jobs of the future:													
Invest in R&D and the technologies of the future:													
Advance U.S. leadership in critical technologies and upgrade America's research infrastructure:													
Fund research infrastructure, including Historically Black Colleges and Universities (HBCU) set-aside	....	2,000	5,800	7,200	7,400	7,100	5,540	2,740	1,340	640	240	29,500	40,000
Increase research and development for existing programs	....	600	2,100	3,600	5,100	6,630	6,090	3,090	1,590	840	360	18,030	30,000
Transform the National Science Foundation by adding a technology directorate	....	1,200	4,000	6,400	8,600	10,760	9,720	4,920	2,520	1,320	560	30,960	50,000
Establish the United States as a leader in climate science, innovation, and R&D:													
Increase climate-focused research	....	100	400	800	1,250	1,230	630	330	180	80	....	3,780	5,000
Increase demonstration funding at energy programs	....	500	1,250	3,250	4,000	3,750	1,750	500	....	....	....	12,750	15,000
Launch Advanced Research Projects Agency-Climate	....	600	2,100	2,700	3,000	3,000	2,400	900	300	....	....	11,400	15,000
Eliminate racial and gender inequities in research and development and science, technology, engineering, and math:													
Fund research and development grants at HBCUs/Minority Serving Institutions (MSIs)	....	200	700	1,200	1,700	2,210	2,030	1,030	530	280	120	6,010	10,000
Create Science, Technology, Engineering, Math (STEM) centers of excellence	....	200	700	1,200	1,700	2,210	2,030	1,030	530	280	120	6,010	10,000
Fund STEM education and training	....	160	500	720	880	1,018	886	446	226	116	48	3,278	5,000
Total, invest in R&D and the technologies of the future	....	5,560	17,550	27,070	33,630	37,908	31,076	14,986	7,216	3,556	1,448	121,718	180,000
Retool and revitalize American manufacturers and small businesses:													
Strengthen manufacturing supply chains for critical goods:													
Create a Critical Supply Chain Resilience Fund	....	5,000	10,000	20,000	10,000	5,000	....	....	....	....	....	50,000	50,000
Provide incentives for semiconductor manufacturing and research	....	750	4,000	7,750	12,000	13,000	8,500	4,000	....	....	....	37,500	50,000
Prepare Americans for future pandemics	....	1,650	6,485	7,145	7,520	5,815	995	390	....	....	....	28,615	30,000
Prepare Americans for future pandemics—Department of Health and Human Services (HHS) (non-add)	....	1,620	5,100	5,640	6,000	4,380	900	360	....	....	....	22,740	24,000
Prepare Americans for future pandemics—Department of Defense (non-add)	....	....	1,250	1,250	1,250	1,250	....	....	....	....	....	5,000	5,000
Prepare Americans for future pandemics—Department of Energy (non-add)	....	30	135	255	270	185	95	30	....	....	....	875	1,000

Table S–6. Mandatory and Receipt Proposals—Continued

(Deficit increases (+) or decreases (−) in millions of dollars)

	2021	2022	2023	2024	2025	2026	2027	2028	2029	2030	2031	Totals 2022–2026	Totals 2022–2031
Jumpstart clean energy manufacturing through Federal procurement:													
Procure advanced nuclear power	......	100	150	250	500	2,500	1,250	250	......	......	......	3,500	5,000
Procure low carbon materials	......	400	1,800	2,200	2,900	3,000	3,000	2,400	300	......	......	10,300	16,000
Electrify the Federal vehicle fleet and support the necessary charging infrastructure	......	250	250	500	1,000	1,000	1,000	1,000	......	......	......	3,000	5,000
Electrify the Postal Service fleet	......	800	800	800	......	......	......	......	......	......	......	2,400	2,400
Procure carbon-free power and sustainable buildings	......	400	2,000	3,200	4,000	4,000	3,600	2,000	800	......	......	13,600	20,000
Make it in all of America:													
Expand Manufacturing USA	......	300	600	1,200	600	300	......	......	......	......	......	3,000	3,000
Invest in research at the National Institute of Standards and Technology (NIST) labs	......	800	800	800	800	800	......	......	......	......	......	4,000	4,000
Expand the Manufacturing Extension Partnership	......	700	1,400	2,800	1,400	700	......	......	......	......	......	7,000	7,000
Establish regional innovation hubs	......	3,500	1,500	3,500	750	750	......	......	......	......	......	10,000	10,000
Invest in a community revitalization fund	......	......	20	80	360	660	1,020	1,400	1,920	1,640	1,340	1,120	8,440
Increase access to capital for domestic manufacturers:													
Modernize the auto supply chain	......	1,100	3,300	4,950	5,500	4,400	2,200	550	......	......	......	19,250	22,000
Establish a manufacturing financing facility	......	3,650	3,050	3,055	50	45	40	35	30	25	20	9,850	10,000
Finance clean energy manufacturing	......	80	400	640	800	800	720	400	160	......	......	2,720	4,000
Increase business and industry guaranteed loans	......	220	200	55	20	5	......	......	......	......	......	500	500
Increase biorefinery, renewable chemical and biobased product manufacturing	......	4,930	4,060	3,190	1,740	580	......	......	......	......	......	14,500	14,500
Support U.S. companies abroad and mobilize private sector investment to counter climate change—U.S. Development Finance Corporation	......	51	80	100	100	100	100	49	20	......	......	431	600
Develop vibrant global markets to support U.S. job creation—USAID Development Assistance Program	......	12	32	56	72	80	68	48	24	8	......	252	400
Create a national network of small business incubators and innovation hubs:													
Support small business manufacturing through the Small Business Administration	......	1,500	1,875	2,250	2,625	3,750	4,875	6,000	7,125	......	......	12,000	30,000
Support small business manufacturing through the Minority Business Development Agency	......	100	100	100	100	100	100	100	100	100	100	500	1,000
Partner with rural and Tribal communities to create jobs and economic growth in rural America:													
Create a new rural partnership fund	......	650	1,050	1,500	1,650	150	......	......	......	......	......	5,000	5,000
Total, retool and revitalize American manufacturers and small businesses	......	26,943	43,952	66,121	54,487	47,535	27,468	18,622	10,479	1,773	1,460	239,038	298,840
Invest in workforce development:													
Pair job creation efforts with next generation training programs:													
Scale Sectoral Employment through Career Training for Occupational Readiness (SECTOR)	......	......	196	1,288	1,944	2,200	2,372	2,400	2,400	2,400	2,400	5,628	17,600

Table S-6. Mandatory and Receipt Proposals—Continued

(Deficit increases (+) or decreases (−) in millions of dollars)

	2021	2022	2023	2024	2025	2026	2027	2028	2029	2030	2031	Totals 2022–2026	Totals 2022–2031
Provide Comprehensive Supports for Dislocated Workers (CSDW)		234	1,638	1,800	1,800	1,800	1,800	1,800	1,800	1,800	1,800	7,272	16,272
Target workforce development opportunities in underserved communities:													
Support subsidized jobs		600	600	400	400	400	400	300	300	300	300	2,400	4,000
Support the phase out of 14(c)		300	400	400	400	300	200	....	....	....	....	1,800	2,000
Expand reentry training and violence prevention efforts		....	45	70	85	100	100	100	100	100	100	300	800
Invest in community violence intervention		....	15	100	260	420	570	685	795	880	720	795	4,445
Community violence intervention–Department of Justice (non-add)		....	8	50	130	210	285	343	398	440	360	398	2,223
Community violence intervention–HHS (non-add)		....	8	50	130	210	285	343	398	440	360	398	2,223
Build the capacity of the existing workforce development and worker protection systems:													
Expand adult education		5	70	95	100	100	100	100	100	100	100	370	870
Bolster Department of Labor enforcement		....	200	375	560	740	905	1,050	1,175	1,235	1,260	1,875	7,500
Bolster Equal Employment Opportunity Commission enforcement		....	46	67	92	117	133	175	237	296	337	322	1,500
Bolster National Labor Relations Board enforcement		....	36	43	60	76	93	114	157	193	228	215	1,000
Expand career pathways for middle and high school students		50	700	950	1,000	1,000	1,000	1,000	1,000	1,000	1,000	3,700	8,700
Expand career services		80	752	800	800	800	800	800	800	800	800	3,232	7,232
Fund community college training partnerships		....	70	280	510	780	850	950	1,010	1,060	1,050	1,640	6,560
Scale Registered Apprenticeship and pre-apprenticeship		....	112	716	972	1,014	1,086	1,100	1,100	1,086	1,014	2,814	8,200
Total, invest in workforce development		1,269	4,880	7,384	8,983	9,847	10,409	10,574	10,974	11,250	11,109	32,363	86,679
Total, invest in R&D, revitalize manufacturing and small businesses, and train Americans for the jobs of the future		33,772	66,382	100,575	97,100	95,290	68,953	44,182	28,669	16,579	14,017	393,119	565,519
Made in America Tax Plan:													
Prioritize clean energy:													
Eliminate fossil fuel tax preferences:													
Repeal enhanced oil recovery credit		−158	−389	−599	−808	−951	−988	−980	−975	−974	−976	−2,905	−7,798
Repeal deduction for tertiary injectants		....	....	....	....	....	....	....	....	....	....	....	....
Repeal credit for oil and gas produced from marginal wells		−39	−100	−128	−116	−78	−38	−14	−3	....	....	−461	−516
Repeal expensing of intangible drilling costs		−2,182	−1,954	−1,569	−1,174	−747	−562	−586	−591	−585	−536	−7,626	−10,486
Repeal exemption to passive loss limitation for working interests in oil and natural gas		−10	−10	−9	−9	−9	−8	−8	−8	−8	−7	−47	−86
Repeal percentage depletion for oil and natural gas wells		−678	−767	−794	−831	−890	−946	−996	−1,045	−1,093	−1,132	−3,960	−9,172
Repeal amortization of air pollution control equipment		−16	−39	−60	−80	−99	−117	−134	−132	−119	−105	−294	−901

Table S–6. Mandatory and Receipt Proposals—Continued

(Deficit increases (+) or decreases (–) in millions of dollars)

	2021	2022	2023	2024	2025	2026	2027	2028	2029	2030	2031	Totals 2022–2026	Totals 2022–2031
Increase geological and geophysical amortization period for independent producer	.....	–38	–139	–227	–247	–246	–242	–233	–217	–201	–195	–897	–1,985
Repeal expensing of exploration and development costs	.....	–190	–170	–136	–102	–65	–49	–51	–51	–51	–46	–663	–911
Repeal percentage depletion for hard mineral fossil fuels	.....	–97	–110	–114	–119	–127	–136	–142	–149	–156	–161	–567	–1,311
Repeal capital gains treatment for royalties	.....	–46	–47	–48	–49	–51	–52	–50	–44	–37	–31	–241	–455
Treat publicly traded partnerships as C corporations	.....	.....	.....	.....	.....	.....	–83	–169	–216	–259	–300	.....	–1,027
Excise tax exemption for crude oil derived from bitumen and kerogen-rich rock	.....	–31	–39	–39	–39	–39	–40	–41	–41	–42	–44	–187	–395
Total, eliminate fossil fuel tax preferences	.....	–3,485	–3,764	–3,723	–3,574	–3,302	–3,261	–3,404	–3,472	–3,525	–3,533	–17,848	–35,043
Extend and enhance renewable and alternative energy incentives:													
Extend and modify the Energy Investment Credit[1]	.....	1,397	5,767	26,324	30,423	31,149	35,455	26,833	23,061	18,540	11,642	95,060	210,591
Extend and modify the Renewable Energy Production Tax Credit[1]	.....	2,059	2,106	937	1,429	1,903	2,780	4,606	6,267	7,730	8,802	8,434	38,619
Extend and modify the Residential Efficient Property Credit	.....	290	480	1,594	2,256	2,538	2,846	2,425	1,933	1,342	392	7,158	16,096
Total, extend and enhance renewable and alternative energy incentives	.....	3,746	8,353	28,855	34,108	35,590	41,081	33,864	31,261	27,612	20,836	110,652	265,306
Provide tax credit for electricity transmission investments[1]	.....	187	250	1,746	2,280	2,863	3,118	3,239	3,246	3,420	3,447	7,326	23,796
Provide allocated credit for electricity generation from existing nuclear power facilities[1]	.....	750	1,000	1,000	1,000	1,000	1,000	1,000	1,000	1,000	1,000	4,750	9,750
Establish new tax credits for qualifying advanced energy manufacturing[1]	.....	425	1,102	1,492	988	824	940	1,396	576	58	131	4,831	7,932
Establish tax credits for heavy- and medium-duty zero emission vehicles[1]	.....	71	295	835	1,471	2,692	4,028	1,178	63	11	.....	5,364	10,644
Provide tax incentives for sustainable aviation fuel	.....	363	503	633	693	1,313	1,696	743	376	199	117	3,505	6,636
Provide a production tax credit for low-carbon hydrogen[1]	.....	14	53	156	358	548	979	1,570	445	5	.....	1,129	4,128
Extend and enhance energy efficiency and electrification incentives:													
Extend and modify the nonbusiness energy property credit	.....	532	1,806	2,460	1,940	1,056	634	.....	.....	.....	.....	7,794	8,428
Extend and increase the tax credit for manufacturing credit for new energy efficient new homes	.....	128	271	298	313	337	220	72	25	8	2	1,347	1,674
Extend and increase the commercial buildings deduction	.....	146	280	328	346	350	350	350	350	351	354	1,450	3,205
Provide tax credits for the installation of mechanical insulation	.....	317	606	736	867	1,007	737	454	344	229	110	3,533	5,407
Total, extend and enhance energy efficiency and electrification incentives	.....	1,123	2,963	3,822	3,466	2,750	1,941	876	719	588	466	14,124	18,714
Provide disaster mitigation tax credit	.....	391	411	415	415	415	415	415	415	415	332	2,047	4,039
Extend and enhance the Carbon Oxide Sequestration Credit[1]	.....	21	10	10	19	27	101	101	53	2,082	3,634	87	6,058

Table S–6. Mandatory and Receipt Proposals—Continued

(Deficit increases (+) or decreases (–) in millions of dollars)

	2021	2022	2023	2024	2025	2026	2027	2028	2029	2030	2031	Totals 2022–2026	Totals 2022–2031
Extend and enhance the electric vehicle charging station credit [1]	......	236	432	848	1,457	2,599	771	18	–26	–35	–33	5,572	6,267
Modify Oil Spill Liability Trust Fund financing	......	–38	–51	–53	–53	–53	–53	–53	–53	–53	–53	–248	–513
Reinstate Superfund excise taxes	......	–1,715	–2,340	–2,406	–2,455	–2,517	–2,560	–2,610	–2,670	–2,723	–2,787	–11,433	–24,783
Revenue effect of sparking widespread adoption of EVs	......	10	32	66	113	178	267	409	647	1,022	1,584	399	4,328
Total, prioritize clean energy	......	2,099	9,249	33,696	40,286	44,927	50,463	38,742	32,580	30,076	25,141	130,257	307,259
Reform corporate taxation:													
Increase the domestic corporate tax rate to 28 percent	......	–51,127	–86,182	–88,059	–89,385	–91,784	–92,065	–90,730	–89,357	–88,798	–90,330	–406,537	–857,817
Revise the Global Minimum Tax regime, disallow deductions attributable to exempt income, and limit inversions	......	–29,816	–51,386	–54,192	–57,030	–55,283	–54,699	–56,056	–56,988	–58,223	–59,830	–247,707	–533,503
Reform taxation of foreign fossil fuel income:													
Modify foreign oil and gas extraction income (FOGEI) and foreign oil related income (FORI) rules	......	–4,178	–7,173	–7,468	–7,834	–8,393	–9,055	–9,633	–10,051	–10,358	–10,638	–35,046	–84,781
Modify tax rule for dual capacity taxpayers	......	–48	–123	–128	–134	–143	–154	–165	–173	–178	–183	–576	–1,429
Total, reform taxation of foreign fossil fuel income	......	–4,226	–7,296	–7,596	–7,968	–8,536	–9,209	–9,798	–10,224	–10,536	–10,821	–35,622	–86,210
Provide tax incentives for locating jobs and business activity in the United States and remove tax deductions for shipping jobs overseas:													
Provide tax credit for onshoring jobs to the United States	......	6	10	10	11	11	12	12	13	13	14	48	112
Remove tax deductions for shipping jobs overseas	......	–6	–10	–10	–11	–11	–12	–12	–13	–13	–14	–48	–112
Total, provide tax incentives for locating jobs and business activity in the United States and remove tax deductions for shipping jobs overseas	......	......	......	......	......	......	......	......	......	......	......	......	......
Repeal deduction for Foreign Derived Intangible Income (FDII) and provide additional support for research and experimentation expenditures	......	......	......	......	......	......	......	......	......	......	......	......	......
Replace the Base Erosion Anti-Abuse Tax (BEAT) with the Stopping Harmful Inversions and Ending Low-Tax Developments (SHIELD) Rule	......	......	–33,244	–53,796	–51,111	–47,655	–44,463	–41,914	–39,425	–38,990	–39,453	–185,806	–390,051
Limit foreign tax credits for sales of hybrid entities	......	–23	–39	–41	–43	–45	–47	–48	–49	–50	–51	–191	–436
Restrict deductions of excessive interest of members of financial reporting groups for disproportionate borrowing in the United States	......	–2,100	–2,334	–1,586	–1,638	–1,690	–1,743	–1,795	–1,846	–1,900	–1,956	–9,348	–18,588
Impose 15 percent minimum tax on book earnings of large corporations	......	–10,736	–15,245	–14,588	–13,812	–14,561	–15,203	–16,049	–16,158	–15,775	–16,217	–68,942	–148,344
Total, reform corporate taxation	......	–98,028	–195,726	–219,858	–220,987	–219,554	–217,429	–216,390	–214,047	–214,272	–218,658	–954,153	–2,034,949
Support housing and infrastructure:													
Expand Low-income Housing Tax Credit	......	35	212	707	1,592	2,527	3,427	4,370	5,362	6,339	7,356	5,073	31,927
Provide Neighborhood Homes Investment Tax Credit	......	10	99	398	944	1,512	1,889	2,063	2,083	2,035	2,001	2,963	13,034

Table S–6. Mandatory and Receipt Proposals—Continued

(Deficit increases (+) or decreases (−) in millions of dollars)

	2021	2022	2023	2024	2025	2026	2027	2028	2029	2030	2031	Totals 2022–2026	Totals 2022–2031
Expand New Markets Tax Credit (NMTC) and make permanent	....	....	....	....	....	97	280	492	736	1,006	1,294	97	3,905
Provide federally subsidized State and local bonds for infrastructure including for schools[1]	....	291	767	1,292	1,458	1,439	1,403	1,357	1,308	1,257	1,204	5,247	11,776
Total, support housing and infrastructure	....	336	1,078	2,397	3,994	5,575	6,999	8,282	9,489	10,637	11,855	13,380	60,642
Total, Made in America Tax Plan	....	−95,593	−185,399	−183,765	−176,707	−169,052	−159,967	−169,366	−171,978	−173,559	−181,662	−810,516	−1,667,048
Total, American Jobs Plan	....	**83,966**	**91,798**	**140,815**	**151,910**	**176,801**	**109,650**	**28,359**	**−34,570**	**−86,876**	**−132,909**	**645,290**	**528,944**

American Families Plan

Add at least four years of free public education:

Universal preschool:

	2021	2022	2023	2024	2025	2026	2027	2028	2029	2030	2031	Totals 2022–2026	Totals 2022–2031
Provide universal preschool grants to States	....	302	2,203	6,306	9,637	11,158	13,673	16,417	20,323	25,638	33,501	29,606	139,158
Provide Head Start educator fund	....	1,004	2,530	2,580	2,633	2,685	2,738	2,794	2,849	2,906	2,965	11,432	25,684
Free community college and other postsecondary education investments:													
Fund free community college	....	429	9,532	15,399	17,496	12,892	11,053	10,864	10,418	10,092	10,349	55,748	108,524
Account for American Opportunity Tax Credit interaction with free community college[1]	....	−22	−455	−901	−1,354	−1,847	−2,243	−2,662	−3,094	−3,590	−4,031	−4,579	−20,199
Increase the Pell Grant	....	3,550	8,336	8,608	8,664	8,648	8,797	8,987	9,193	9,372	9,558	37,806	83,713
Make Deferred Action for Childhood Arrivals (DACA) recipients eligible for Pell Grants	....	45	146	206	206	187	164	162	136	79	67	790	1,398
Create completion grants for student supports	....	186	4,092	5,828	6,014	6,200	6,200	6,200	6,200	6,200	6,200	22,320	53,320
Fund Advancing Affordability for students	....	139	3,050	4,078	4,180	4,347	4,430	4,567	4,710	4,860	5,016	15,794	39,377
Increase funding to HBCUs/Tribal Colleges and Universities (TCUs)/MSIs in Titles III/V programs	....	15	330	470	485	500	500	500	500	500	500	1,800	4,300
Create or expand health care graduate programs at HBCUs/TCUs/MSIs	....	6	132	188	194	200	200	200	200	200	200	720	1,720
Total, add at least four years of free public education	....	5,654	29,896	42,762	48,155	44,970	45,512	48,029	51,435	56,257	64,325	171,437	436,995
Education and preparation for teachers:													
Expand Teacher Quality Partnerships	....	8	184	263	271	280	280	280	280	280	280	1,006	2,406
Create Hawkins Centers of Excellence	....	1	26	37	39	40	40	40	40	40	40	143	343
Increase Individuals with Disabilities Education Act (IDEA) personnel preparation funding	....	4	80	88	90	90	90	90	90	90	90	352	802
Reform and expand Teacher Education Assistance for College and Higher Education (TEACH) grants	....	24	120	123	125	127	128	130	133	134	136	519	1,180
Invest in teacher credentials	....	32	560	560	400	48	....	....	....	....	....	1,600	1,600
Invest in teacher leadership and development	....	4	74	144	194	200	200	200	200	200	200	616	1,616
Total, education and preparation for teachers	....	73	1,044	1,215	1,119	785	738	740	743	744	746	4,236	7,947
Provide direct support to children and families:													
Establish a new child care program for American families	....	6,720	8,860	11,820	13,760	17,230	20,910	24,480	31,820	40,090	49,270	58,390	224,960
Provide universal paid family and medical leave	....	750	9,355	12,406	13,909	15,362	20,739	25,626	36,438	41,546	48,918	51,782	225,049

Table S–6. Mandatory and Receipt Proposals—Continued

(Deficit increases (+) or decreases (–) in millions of dollars)

	2021	2022	2023	2024	2025	2026	2027	2028	2029	2030	2031	Totals 2022–2026	Totals 2022–2031
Nutrition:													
Expand Summer Electronic Benefit Transfer (Summer EBT) to all eligible children nationwide	......	......	1,446	1,980	2,538	3,123	3,197	3,271	3,348	3,430	3,511	9,087	25,844
Expand school meal programs	......	210	1,662	1,746	1,798	1,847	1,895	1,951	2,007	2,051	2,104	7,263	17,271
Launch a healthy food incentives demonstration	......	1,000	......	......	......	......	......	......	......	......	......	1,000	1,000
Facilitate re-entry for formerly incarcerated individuals through Supplemental Nutrition Assistance Program (SNAP) eligibility	......	106	87	86	84	82	82	85	88	90	92	445	882
Place family coordinators at Veterans Affairs medical centers	......	30	30	25	25	25	25	25	25	25	25	135	260
Invest in maternal health	......	24	180	504	582	600	576	420	96	18	......	1,890	3,000
Total, provide direct support to children and families	......	8,840	21,620	28,567	32,696	38,269	47,424	55,858	73,822	87,250	103,920	129,992	498,266
Support workers and families and strengthen economic security:													
Extend the American Rescue Plan changes to the Child Credit through 2025 and make permanent full refundability[1]	......	47,125	110,999	108,559	107,190	62,060	2,860	2,725	2,611	2,512	2,420	435,933	449,061
Make permanent the American Rescue Plan expansion to Earned Income Tax Credit for workers without qualifying children[1]	......	27	5,589	11,782	11,970	12,145	12,445	12,576	12,745	12,908	13,032	41,513	105,219
Make permanent the American Rescue Plan changes to the Child and Dependent Care Tax Credit (CDCTC)[1]	......	3,134	10,588	10,588	10,633	12,303	11,032	11,195	11,391	11,573	11,761	47,246	104,198
Account for CDCTC interaction with new child care program for American families[1,2]	......	–982	–1,205	–1,437	–1,680	–1,934	–2,199	–2,474	–2,992	–3,531	–4,093	–7,238	–22,527
Make permanent the American Rescue Plan expansion of premium tax credits[1]	......	0	11,490	15,679	16,513	17,215	18,076	18,888	20,149	21,704	23,334	60,897	163,048
Increase the employer-provided childcare tax credit for businesses	......	28	28	29	29	29	31	31	32	32	33	143	302
Total, support workers, families, and economic security	......	49,332	137,489	145,200	144,655	101,818	42,245	42,941	43,936	45,198	46,487	578,494	799,301
Strengthen taxation of high-income taxpayers and close loopholes:													
Increase top marginal tax rate for high earners	......	–19,991	–30,594	–33,278	–36,525	–11,532	......	......	......	......	......	–131,920	–131,920
Reform taxation of capital income	–1,241	–7,656	–25,451	–32,906	–36,303	–33,947	–32,252	–34,276	–36,064	–37,937	–45,693	–136,263	–322,485
Rationalize Net Investment Income and Self-Employment Contributions Act (SECA) taxes	......	–11,383	–19,535	–20,779	–23,038	–24,205	–25,464	–26,719	–27,559	–28,416	–29,402	–98,940	–236,500
Tax carried (profits) interest as ordinary income	......	–100	–135	–138	–141	–143	–149	–155	–162	–169	–176	–657	–1,468
Repeal deferral of gain from like-kind exchanges	......	–676	–1,857	–1,914	–1,971	–2,030	–2,091	–2,154	–2,218	–2,285	–2,354	–8,448	–19,550
Make permanent excess business loss limitation of noncorporate taxpayers	......	......	......	......	......	......	–9,996	–11,782	–7,627	–6,836	–6,619	......	–42,860
Total, strengthen taxation of high-income taxpayers and close loopholes	–1,241	–39,806	–77,572	–89,015	–97,978	–71,857	–69,952	–75,086	–73,630	–75,643	–84,244	–376,228	–754,783

Table S–6. Mandatory and Receipt Proposals—Continued

(Deficit increases (+) or decreases (−) in millions of dollars)

	2021	2022	2023	2024	2025	2026	2027	2028	2029	2030	2031	Totals 2022–2026	Totals 2022–2031
Improve tax compliance and administration:													
Implement a program integrity allocation adjustment and provide additional resources for tax administration:													
Increase revenues through program integrity allocation adjustment for tax administration	......	−334	−1,858	−3,165	−4,055	−4,894	−5,889	−6,595	−7,243	−7,796	−8,451	−14,306	−50,280
Increase revenues by providing mandatory Internal Revenue Service (IRS) funding for compliance	......	0	−631	−3,312	−7,562	−13,837	−22,342	−34,081	−46,941	−62,253	−74,937	−25,342	−265,896
Provide mandatory IRS funding for compliance	......	953	1,959	2,938	4,069	5,441	7,047	9,035	11,222	13,894	14,499	15,360	71,057
Implement a program integrity allocation adjustment for tax administration, discretionary outlays (non-add)	......	375	620	641	657	676	692	710	729	749	767	2,969	6,616
Total, implement a program integrity allocation adjustment and provide additional resources for tax administration	......	619	−530	−3,539	−7,548	−13,290	−21,184	−31,641	−42,962	−56,155	−68,889	−24,288	−245,119
Introduce comprehensive financial account information reporting	......	−8,378	−32,413	−36,551	−42,517	−46,980	−53,032	−57,123	−61,024	−61,886	−62,742	−166,839	−462,646
Increase oversight of paid tax return preparers:													
Allow IRS to regulate paid Federal tax return preparers[1]	......	−35	−52	−57	−59	−58	−55	−57	−61	−68	−73	−261	−575
Increase penalties on ghost preparers[1]	......	−13	−19	−21	−24	−25	−26	−27	−28	−29	−30	−102	−242
Total, increase oversight of paid tax return preparers	......	−48	−71	−78	−83	−83	−81	−84	−89	−97	−103	−363	−817
Enhance accuracy of tax information:													
E-file of forms and returns	......	......	......	......	......	......	......	......	......	......	......	......	......
Taxpayer Identification Numbers certification for reportable payments	......	−36	−83	−141	−193	−202	−211	−221	−231	−241	−252	−655	−1,811
Total, enhance accuracy of tax information	......	−36	−83	−141	−193	−202	−211	−221	−231	−241	−252	−655	−1,811
Expand broker information reporting with respect to cryptocurrency assets	......	......	......	......	......	......	......	......	......	......	......	......	......
Address taxpayer noncompliance:													
Extend statute of limitation	......	−23	−52	−66	−79	−77	−76	−74	−73	−71	−70	−297	−661
Impose liability on shareholders to collect unpaid income taxes of applicable corporations	......	−395	−412	−428	−444	−462	−479	−498	−518	−539	−560	−2,141	−4,735
Total, address taxpayer noncompliance	......	−418	−464	−494	−523	−539	−555	−572	−591	−610	−630	−2,438	−5,396
Modify tax administration rules:													
Amend centralized partnership audit regime (BBA) to provide for the carryover of non-refundable reporting year amounts that exceed the income tax liability of a partner	......	5	5	5	5	6	6	7	7	7	7	26	60
Modify requisite supervisory approval of penalty included in notice	......	−29	−254	−245	−248	−222	−197	−174	−173	−179	−186	−998	−1,907
Total, modify tax administration rules	......	−24	−249	−240	−243	−216	−191	−167	−166	−172	−179	−972	−1,847

Table S–6. Mandatory and Receipt Proposals—Continued

(Deficit increases (+) or decreases (−) in millions of dollars)

	2021	2022	2023	2024	2025	2026	2027	2028	2029	2030	2031	Totals 2022–2026	Totals 2022–2031
Authorize limited sharing of business tax return information to measure the economy more accurately													
Increase Low Income Taxpayer Clinic (LITC) grant cap and index it for inflation													
Total, improve tax compliance and administration		−8,285	−33,810	−41,043	−51,107	−61,310	−75,254	−89,808	−105,063	−119,161	−132,795	−195,555	−717,636
Total, American Families Plan	−1,241	15,808	78,667	87,686	77,540	52,675	−9,287	−17,326	−8,757	−5,355	−1,561	312,376	270,090
Mandatory effects of discretionary proposals													
Increase the Pell Grant discretionary award by $400			72	153	135	134	134	138	142	142	147	494	1,197
Reclassifications:													
Reclassify contract support costs Indian Health Service (IHS)			1,142	1,165	1,188	1,212	1,236	1,261	1,286	1,312	1,338	4,707	11,140
Reclassify contract support costs Bureau of Indian Affairs (BIA)			205	344	354	365	376	387	394	403	411	1,268	3,239
Reclassify Tribal lease payments (IHS)			150	153	156	159	162	166	169	172	176	618	1,463
Reclassify Tribal lease payments (BIA)			38	39	40	40	41	42	43	44	45	157	372
Reclassify Tribal Water Settlements			115	197	245	250	255	260	265	272	277	807	2,136
Program integrity proposals:													
Capturing savings to Medicare and Medicaid from Health Care Fraud and Abuse Control (HCFAC) allocation adjustment		−1,086	−1,144	−1,204	−1,268	−1,304	−1,339	−1,378	−1,415	−1,455	−1,495	−6,006	−13,088
Implement HCFAC allocation adjustment, discretionary outlays (non-add)		*556*	*571*	*587*	*604*	*621*	*638*	*656*	*674*	*693*	*712*	*2,939*	*6,312*
Net effect of HCFAC allocation adjustment (non-add)		*−530*	*−573*	*−617*	*−664*	*−683*	*−701*	*−722*	*−741*	*−762*	*−783*	*−3,067*	*−6,776*
Capturing savings to Unemployment Insurance from Reemployment Services and Eligibility Assessment (RESEA) allocation adjustment[3]		−290	−512	−716	−545	−935	−866	−763	−657	−319	−572	−2,998	−6,175
Implement RESEA allocation adjustment, discretionary outlays (non-add)		*130*	*252*	*424*	*528*	*605*	*631*	*646*	*658*	*671*	*685*	*1,939*	*5,230*
Net effect of RESEA allocation adjustment (non-add)		*−160*	*−260*	*−292*	*−17*	*−330*	*−235*	*−117*	*1*	*352*	*113*	*−1,059*	*−945*
Capturing savings from Social Security Administration (SSA) allocation adjustment[4]		−245	−2,529	−3,428	−4,497	−5,291	−6,058	−7,186	−7,282	−8,356	−9,084	−15,990	−53,956
Implement SSA allocation adjustment, discretionary outlays (non-add)		*1,599*	*1,653*	*1,726*	*1,583*	*1,593*	*1,654*	*1,659*	*1,692*	*1,724*	*1,760*	*8,154*	*16,643*
Net effect of SSA allocation adjustment (non-add)		*1,354*	*−876*	*−1,702*	*−2,914*	*−3,698*	*−4,404*	*−5,527*	*−5,590*	*−6,632*	*−7,324*	*−7,836*	*−37,313*
Total, mandatory effects of discretionary proposals		−1,621	−2,463	−3,297	−4,192	−5,370	−6,059	−7,073	−7,055	−7,785	−8,757	−16,943	−53,672
Total, mandatory and receipt proposals	−1,241	98,153	168,002	225,204	225,258	224,106	94,304	3,960	−50,382	−100,016	−143,227	940,723	745,362

[1] The estimates for this proposal include effects on outlays. The outlay effects included in the totals above are as follows:

	2021	2022	2023	2024	2025	2026	2027	2028	2029	2030	2031	Totals 2022–2026	Totals 2022–2031
Extend and Modify the Renewable Energy Production Tax Credit		3,416	4,582	4,703	5,895	6,530	7,167	8,574	9,749	10,557	10,895	25,126	72,068

Table S–6. Mandatory and Receipt Proposals—Continued

(Deficit increases (+) or decreases (−) in millions of dollars)

	2021	2022	2023	2024	2025	2026	2027	2028	2029	2030	2031	Totals 2022–2026	Totals 2022–2031
Provide tax credit for electricity transmission investments	.....	203	270	1,789	2,295	2,801	2,970	3,071	3,105	3,308	3,375	7,358	23,187
Provide allocated credit for electricity generation from existing nuclear power facilities	.....	675	900	900	900	900	900	900	900	900	900	4,275	8,775
Establish new tax credits for qualifying advanced energy manufacturing	.....	385	1,000	1,350	889	735	847	1,261	518	39	117	4,359	7,141
Establish tax credits for heavy- and medium-duty zero emission vehicles	.....	66	272	768	1,346	2,462	3,673	992	.....	.....	.....	4,914	9,579
Provide a production tax credit for low-carbon hydrogen	.....	11	42	128	313	469	839	1,495	419	.....	.....	963	3,716
Extend and enhance the Carbon Oxide Sequestration Credit	.....	547	655	752	939	1,206	2,063	2,767	2,950	5,018	6,520	4,099	23,417
Extend and enhance the electric vehicle charging station credit	.....	158	259	334	412	540	144	.....	.....	.....	.....	1,703	1,847
Provide federally subsidized State and local bonds for infrastructure including for schools	.....	345	964	1,637	1,880	1,819	1,753	1,686	1,620	1,554	1,488	6,645	14,746
Account for American Opportunity Tax Credit interaction with Free Community College	.....	.....	−205	−380	−579	−790	−786	−940	−1,095	−1,271	−1,459	−1,954	−7,505
Extend the American Rescue Plan changes to the Child Credit and make permanent full refundability	.....	80,956	137,868	135,741	134,880	54,147	2,851	2,716	2,602	2,503	2,411	543,592	556,675
Make permanent the American Rescue Plan expansion to Earned Income Tax Credit for workers without children	.....	.....	5,231	10,670	10,839	10,984	11,122	11,018	11,163	11,304	11,409	37,724	93,740
Make permanent the American Rescue Plan changes to the Child and Dependent Care Tax Credit (CDCTC)	.....	.....	6,442	6,455	6,486	6,554	4,694	4,758	4,835	4,908	4,977	25,937	50,109
Account for CDCTC interaction with new child care program for American families	.....	.....	−733	−876	−1,025	−1,030	−936	−1,052	−1,270	−1,497	−1,732	−3,664	−10,151
Make permanent the American Rescue Plan expansion of premium tax credits	.....	.....	8,620	11,666	12,244	12,327	12,768	13,247	14,073	15,052	16,094	44,857	116,091
Allow IRS to regulate paid Federal tax return preparers	.....	−19	−34	−35	−34	−30	−24	−23	−24	−27	−29	−152	−279
Increase penalties on ghost preparers	.....	.....	−2	−2	−3	−3	−3	−3	−3	−3	−3	−10	−25
Total, outlay effects of receipt proposals	.....	90,679	175,151	204,834	211,478	133,642	88,052	79,506	74,073	71,775	67,530	815,784	1,196,720

	2021	2022	2023	2024	2025	2026	2027	2028	2029	2030	2031	Totals 2022–2026	Totals 2022–2031
RESEA allocation adjustment effects	0	0	15	109	399	59	83	117	151	423	109	582	1465

[2] Individuals will not be able to claim both the Child and Dependent Care Tax Credit and participate in the new Child Care for American Families program for the same care. This interaction removes costs already included in the Child Care for American Families score.

[3] The estimates for this proposal include effects on receipts. The receipt effects included in the totals above are as follows:

[4] Represents the savings associated with continuing to provide dedicated funding, through a discretionary allocation adjustment, for program integrity activities to confirm program participants remain eligible to receive benefits.

Table S–7. Funding Levels for Appropriated ("Discretionary") Programs by Category

(Budget authority in billions of dollars)

	Enacted[1] 2021	Request 2022	2023	2024	2025	2026	2027	2028	2029	2030	2031	Totals 2022–2026	2022–2031
Base Discretionary Funding Allocation	1,401.3	1,522.5	1,555.2	1,589.5	1,624.7	1,660.8	1,687.5	1,714.7	1,742.4	1,770.5	1,799.3	7,952.6	16,666.9
Defense Allocation[2]	740.7	752.9	769.5	786.6	804.0	821.9	830.1	838.4	846.8	855.3	863.8	3,934.9	8,163.3
Non-Defense Allocation	660.7	769.6	785.7	802.9	820.6	838.9	857.4	876.2	895.6	915.3	935.5	4,017.7	8,497.6
Proposed Growth in Base Discretionary Programs:													
Total		+8.6%	+2.1%	+2.2%	+2.2%	+2.2%	+1.6%	+1.6%	+1.6%	+1.6%	+1.6%		
Defense Allocation		+1.6%	+2.2%	+2.2%	+2.2%	+2.2%	+1.0%	+1.0%	+1.0%	+1.0%	+1.0%		
Non-Defense Allocation		+16.5%	+2.1%	+2.2%	+2.2%	+2.2%	+2.2%	+2.2%	+2.2%	+2.2%	+2.2%		
Non-Defense Reclassifications[3]	....	....	–1.9	–2.0	–2.0	–2.0	–2.1	–2.1	–2.2	–2.2	–2.3	–7.9	–18.8
Indian Water Rights Settlement Funding			–0.2	–0.2	–0.2	–0.3	–0.3	–0.3	–0.3	–0.3	–0.3	–1.0	–2.3
Section 105(l) Leases			–0.2	–0.2	–0.2	–0.2	–0.2	–0.2	–0.2	–0.2	–0.2	–0.8	–1.8
Contract Support Costs			–1.5	–1.5	–1.6	–1.6	–1.6	–1.7	–1.7	–1.7	–1.8	–6.2	–14.6
Non-Base Discretionary Funding (not included above):[4]													
Change in Mandatory Program Offsets	–26.0	–26.0	....	....	....	....	....	....	....	....	....	–26.0	–26.0
Emergency and COVID–19 Supplemental Funding	194.9												
Program Integrity	1.9	2.5	3.1	3.4	3.4	3.5	3.6	3.7	3.8	3.8	3.9	15.9	34.8
Disaster Relief	17.3	18.9	10.1	10.1	10.1	10.1	10.1	10.1	10.1	10.1	10.1	59.5	110.3
Wildfire Suppression	2.4	2.5	2.5	2.5	2.5	2.5	2.5	2.5	2.5	2.5	2.5	12.3	24.5
21st Century Cures Appropriations	0.5	0.5	1.1	0.5	0.2	0.2						2.5	2.5
Total, Non-Base Funding	191.0	–1.5	16.9	16.4	16.1	16.3	16.2	16.3	16.4	16.4	16.5	64.3	146.1
Grand Total, Discretionary Budget Authority	1,592.3	1,521.0	1,570.2	1,604.0	1,638.8	1,675.0	1,701.7	1,728.8	1,756.6	1,784.8	1,813.5	8,009.0	16,794.3

[1] The 2021 enacted level includes changes that occur after appropriations are enacted that are part of budget execution such as transfers, reestimates, and the rebasing as mandatory any changes in mandatory programs (CHIMPs) enacted in appropriations bills. The 2021 levels are adjusted to include OMB's scoring of CHIMPs enacted in 2021 appropriations Acts for a better illustrative comparison with the 2022 request.

[2] The 2023 Budget will be accompanied by a Future Years Defense Program that reflects this Administration's policy judgments and National Security and National Defense strategies. Because these strategy documents are currently under development, out-year defense funding levels in the 2022 budget are mechanical extrapolations. After 2022, defense programs are provided with current services growth through 2026 followed by one-percent increases through 2031, a proxy for long-run efficiencies the Administration believes may be achieved in the defense budget.

[3] The 2022 Budget proposes two reclassifications of programs that historically have been funded as discretionary. This first proposal reclassifies the appropriations for the Contract Support Costs and Section 105(l) lease accounts in the Department of Health and Human Services' Indian Health Service and the Department of the Interior's (DOI) Bureau of Indian Affairs. The second proposal reclassifies DOI's Indian water rights settlements funding. The Budget proposes to offset the increase in mandatory funding resulting from both reclassifications by reducing base discretionary funding by amounts equal to current services inflation of the programs. See the Budget Concepts chapter of the *Analytical Perspectives* volume of the Budget for more information on these proposals.

[4] With the expiration of the discretionary caps in 2022, the Administration's 2022 Budget presents funding differently than under the recent discretionary cap framework. The Administration shifts funds that had been designated as Overseas Contingency Operations (OCO) to the base. Funds for anomalous or above-base activities such as emergency requirements, program integrity, disaster relief, wildfire suppression, and 21st Century Cures appropriations continue to be presented outside of base allocations. In addition, major offsets resulting from proposed changes in mandatory programs are also presented outside of the base.

Table S–8. 2022 Discretionary Request by Major Agency

(Budget authority in billions of dollars)

	2021 Enacted[1]	2022 Request	2022 Request Less 2021 Enacted	
			Dollar	Percent
Base Discretionary Funding:				
Cabinet Departments:				
Agriculture[2]	23.9	27.9	+4.0	+16.7%
Commerce	8.9	11.5	+2.6	+29.4%
Defense	703.7	715.0	+11.3	+1.6%
Education	73.0	102.8	+29.8	+40.8%
Energy (DOE)[3]	41.8	46.2	+4.3	+10.4%
Health and Human Services (HHS)[4]	108.4	133.7	+25.3	+23.4%
Homeland Security (DHS):				
DHS program level	*54.9*	*54.9*	*+**	*+0.1%*
Transportation Security Administration Fees	*−0.5*	*−2.7*	*−2.3*	*N/A*
Housing and Urban Development (HUD):				
HUD program level	*59.6*	*68.7*	*+9.0*	*+15.2%*
HUD receipts	*−15.1*	*−10.5*	*+4.6*	*N/A*
Interior	15.0	17.4	+2.5	+16.7%
Justice	33.5	35.3	+1.8	+5.3%
Labor	12.5	14.2	+1.7	+14.0%
State and International Programs[2,5]	57.3	63.6	+6.3	+11.0%
Transportation (DOT):				
DOT Discretionary Programs	*22.4*	*25.7*	*+3.3*	*+14.8%*
DOT General Fund Transfer to Mandatory Programs[6]	*2.9*	*..........*	*−2.9*	*N/A*
Treasury[5]	13.5	15.0	+1.5	+11.3%
Veterans Affairs	104.6	113.1	+8.5	+8.2%
Major Agencies:				
Corps of Engineers (Corps)[7]	7.8	6.8	−1.0	−12.9%
Environmental Protection Agency	9.2	11.2	+2.0	+21.6%
General Services Administration	−1.0	1.5	+2.5	N/A
National Aeronautics and Space Administration	23.3	24.8	+1.5	+6.6%
National Science Foundation	8.5	10.2	+1.7	+19.8%
Small Business Administration	0.8	0.9	+0.1	+9.5%
Social Security Administration[4]	9.0	9.8	+0.8	+9.3%
Other Agencies	23.4	25.5	+2.1	+8.8%
Subtotal, Base Discretionary Budget Authority	**1,401.3**	**1,522.5**	**+121.1**	**+8.6%**

Table S–8. 2022 Discretionary Request by Major Agency—Continued

(Budget authority in billions of dollars)

	2021 Enacted[1]	2022 Request	2022 Request Less 2021 Enacted	
			Dollar	Percent
Non-Base Discretionary Funding:				
Changes in mandatory program offsets[8]	-26.0	-26.0	......	......
Emergency Requirements and COVID–19 Supplemental Funding:[9]				
Agriculture	1.0	......	-1.0	N/A
Commerce	0.3	......	-0.3	N/A
Education	81.6	......	-81.6	N/A
Energy	-2.3	......	+2.3	N/A
Health and Human Services	73.8	......	-73.8	N/A
Homeland Security	2.8	......	-2.8	N/A
Housing and Urban Development	0.7	......	-0.7	N/A
Interior	0.4	......	-0.4	N/A
Justice	0.6	......	-0.6	N/A
Labor	0.7	......	-0.7	N/A
State and International Programs	5.3	......	-5.3	N/A
Transportation	27.0	......	-27.0	N/A
Treasury	0.5	......	-0.5	N/A
Small Business Administration	2.0	......	-2.0	N/A
Other Agencies	0.4	......	-0.4	N/A
Subtotal, Emergency Requirements	194.9	......	-194.9	N/A
Program Integrity:				
Health and Human Services	0.5	0.6	+0.1	+12.1%
Labor	0.1	0.1	+0.1	+60.2%
Treasury	......	0.4	+0.4	N/A
Social Security Administration	1.3	1.4	+0.1	+10.2%
Subtotal, Program Integrity	1.9	2.5	+0.7	+35.1%
Disaster Relief:				
Homeland Security	17.1	18.8	+1.7	+9.7%
Small Business Administration	0.1	0.1	......	......
Subtotal, Disaster Relief	17.3	18.9	+1.7	+9.6%
Wildfire Suppression:				
Agriculture	2.0	2.1	+0.1	+3.9%
Interior	0.3	0.3	+*	+6.5%
Subtotal, Wildfire Suppression	2.4	2.5	+0.1	+4.3%

Table S–8. 2022 Discretionary Request by Major Agency—Continued

(Budget authority in billions of dollars)

	2021 Enacted[1]	2022 Request	2022 Request Less 2021 Enacted	
			Dollar	Percent
21st Century Cures appropriations:				
Health and Human Services	0.5	0.5	+0.1	+15.2%
Subtotal, Non-Base Discretionary Funding	191.0	–1.5	–192.5	–100.8%
Total, Discretionary Budget Authority	1,592.3	1,521.0	–71.3	–4.5%

* $50 million or less.

[1] The 2021 enacted level includes changes that occur after appropriations are enacted that are part of budget execution such as transfers, reestimates, and the rebasing as mandatory any changes in mandatory programs (CHIMPs) enacted in appropriations bills. The 2021 levels are adjusted to include OMB's scoring of CHIMPs enacted in 2021 appropriations Acts for a better illustrative comparison with the 2022 request.

[2] Funding for Food for Peace Title II Grants is included in the State and International Programs total. Although the funds are appropriated to the Department of Agriculture, the funds are administered by the U.S. Agency for International Development (USAID).

[3] The Department of Energy base total in 2021 includes an appropriation of $2.3 billion that had been designated as emergency in Public Law 116-260 since the activities were for regular operations and not emergency purposes.

[4] Funding from the Hospital Insurance and Supplementary Medical Insurance trust funds for administrative expenses incurred by the Social Security Administration that support the Medicare program are included in the Health and Human Services total and not in the Social Security Administration total.

[5] The State and International Programs total includes funding for the Department of State, USAID, Treasury International, and 11 international agencies while the Treasury total excludes Treasury's International Programs.

[6] The DOT General Fund Transfer to Mandatory Programs line reflects General Fund appropriations to programs that traditionally receive mandatory funding out of the Highway and Airport and Airway Trust Funds.

[7] The 2022 Budget shifts the Formerly Utilized Sites Remedial Action Program (FUSRAP) from the Corps to DOE; setting aside the FUSRAP shift, the change from 2021 is a 10-percent decrease to the Corps non-defense budget.

[8] The limitation enacted and proposed in the Justice Department's Crime Victims Fund program and cancellations in the Children's Health Insurance Program in HHS make up the bulk of these offsets.

[9] Funding enacted in division N of the Consolidated Appropriations Act, 2021 (Public Law 116-260) for otherwise discretionary programs has been rebased from mandatory and is included here along with other emergency requirements provided in 2021. The division N amounts were not designated as emergency but are considered non-base funding.

Table S–9. Economic Assumptions[1]

(Calendar years)

	Actual 2019	2020	2021	2022	2023	2024	Projections						
							2025	2026	2027	2028	2029	2030	2031
Gross Domestic Product (GDP):													
Nominal level, billions of dollars	21,433	20,933	22,411	23,799	24,808	25,778	26,767	27,794	28,860	29,986	31,166	32,414	33,723
Percent change, nominal GDP, year/year	4.0	–2.3	7.1	6.2	4.2	3.9	3.8	3.8	3.8	3.9	3.9	4.0	4.0
Real GDP, percent change, year/year	2.2	–3.5	5.2	4.3	2.2	1.9	1.8	1.8	1.8	1.9	1.9	2.0	2.0
Real GDP, percent change, Q4/Q4	2.3	–2.5	5.2	3.2	2.0	1.8	1.8	1.8	1.8	1.9	1.9	2.0	2.0
GDP chained price index, percent change, year/year	1.8	1.2	1.8	1.9	2.0	2.0	2.0	2.0	2.0	2.0	2.0	2.0	2.0
Consumer Price Index,[2] percent change, year/year	1.8	1.2	2.1	2.1	2.2	2.2	2.3	2.3	2.3	2.3	2.3	2.3	2.3
Interest rates, percent:[3]													
91-day Treasury bills[4]	2.1	0.4	0.1	0.2	0.4	0.8	1.2	1.5	1.6	1.7	1.8	2.1	2.2
10-year Treasury notes	2.1	0.9	1.2	1.4	1.7	2.1	2.4	2.6	2.7	2.8	2.8	2.8	2.8
Unemployment rate, civilian, percent[3]	3.7	8.1	5.5	4.1	3.8	3.8	3.8	3.8	3.8	3.8	3.8	3.8	3.8

Note: A more detailed table of economic assumptions appears in Chapter 2, "Economic Assumptions and Overview," in the *Analytical Perspectives* volume of the Budget.
[1] Based on information available as of mid-February 2021.
[2] Seasonally adjusted CPI for all urban consumers.
[3] Annual average.
[4] Average rate, secondary market (bank discount basis).

Table S–10. Federal Government Financing and Debt

(Dollar amounts in billions)

	Actual 2020	Estimate 2021	2022	2023	2024	2025	2026	2027	2028	2029	2030	2031
Financing:												
Unified budget deficit:												
Primary deficit	2,784	3,366	1,532	1,052	991	1,025	890	701	749	562	649	654
Net interest	345	303	305	320	368	445	524	603	674	744	829	914
Unified budget deficit	3,129	3,669	1,837	1,372	1,359	1,470	1,414	1,303	1,424	1,307	1,477	1,568
As a percent of GDP	14.9%	16.7%	7.8%	5.6%	5.3%	5.5%	5.1%	4.6%	4.8%	4.2%	4.6%	4.7%
Other transactions affecting borrowing from the public:												
Changes in financial assets and liabilities:[1]												
Change in Treasury operating cash balance	1,399	–1,032	....	....	....	....	....	....	....	....	....	....
Net disbursements of credit financing accounts:												
Direct loan and Troubled Asset Relief Program (TARP) equity purchase accounts	198	159	110	44	17	4	3	1	–2	–4	5	8
Guaranteed loan accounts	–499	354	154	5	6	5	5	6	5	5	5	5
Net purchases of non-Federal securities by the National Railroad Retirement Investment Trust (NRRIT)	–*	*	–2	–2	–2	–2	–2	–2	–2	–2	–1	–1
Net change in other financial assets and liabilities[2]	–11	....	....	....	....	....	....	....	....	....	....	....
Subtotal, changes in financial assets and liabilities	1,087	–518	262	47	21	7	6	5	2	–1	8	11
Seigniorage on coins	–*	–1	–*	–1	–1	–1	–1	–1	–1	–1	–1	–1
Total, other transactions affecting borrowing from the public	1,087	–519	261	46	20	7	5	5	1	–1	7	11
Total, requirement to borrow from the public (equals change in debt held by the public)	4,216	3,150	2,098	1,418	1,379	1,476	1,419	1,308	1,425	1,305	1,485	1,578
Changes in Debt Subject to Statutory Limitation:												
Change in debt held by the public	4,216	3,150	2,098	1,418	1,379	1,476	1,419	1,308	1,425	1,305	1,485	1,578
Change in debt held by Government accounts	17	173	121	163	202	106	65	–93	–209	–120	–234	–273
Change in other factors	1	1	1	1	1	–*	*	1	*	*	–1	–1
Total, change in debt subject to statutory limitation	4,234	3,325	2,220	1,582	1,582	1,582	1,485	1,216	1,216	1,185	1,250	1,304
Debt Subject to Statutory Limitation, End of Year:												
Debt issued by Treasury	26,881	30,204	32,423	34,005	35,586	37,167	38,652	39,867	41,083	42,267	43,517	44,821
Adjustment for discount, premium, and coverage[3]	39	41	42	43	44	44	44	45	46	47	47	47
Total, debt subject to statutory limitation[4]	26,920	30,245	32,465	34,048	35,630	37,211	38,696	39,912	41,129	42,314	43,564	44,868
Debt Outstanding, End of Year:												
Gross Federal debt:[5]												
Debt issued by Treasury	26,881	30,204	32,423	34,005	35,586	37,167	38,652	39,867	41,083	42,267	43,517	44,821
Debt issued by other agencies	21	21	22	22	22	22	22	22	22	23	24	25
Total, gross Federal debt	26,902	30,226	32,445	34,026	35,607	37,189	38,673	39,889	41,105	42,290	43,541	44,846
As a percent of GDP	128.1%	137.2%	138.1%	138.5%	139.4%	140.3%	140.5%	139.5%	138.4%	137.0%	135.7%	134.3%

Table S–10. Federal Government Financing and Debt—Continued

(Dollar amounts in billions)

	Actual 2020	Estimate 2021	2022	2023	2024	2025	2026	2027	2028	2029	2030	2031
Held by:												
Debt held by Government accounts	5,886	6,059	6,180	6,343	6,545	6,651	6,716	6,622	6,414	6,294	6,060	5,786
Debt held by the public[6]	21,017	24,167	26,265	27,683	29,062	30,539	31,958	33,266	34,691	35,996	37,481	39,059
As a percent of GDP	100.1%	109.7%	111.8%	112.7%	113.8%	115.2%	116.1%	116.4%	116.8%	116.6%	116.8%	117.0%
Debt Held by the Public Net of Financial Assets:												
Debt held by the public	21,017	24,167	26,265	27,683	29,062	30,539	31,958	33,266	34,691	35,996	37,481	39,059
Less financial assets net of liabilities:												
Treasury operating cash balance	1,782	750	750	750	750	750	750	750	750	750	750	750
Credit financing account balances:												
Direct loan and TARP equity purchase accounts	1,613	1,773	1,883	1,926	1,943	1,947	1,949	1,951	1,949	1,945	1,950	1,957
Guaranteed loan accounts	-467	-112	41	46	52	57	62	68	72	77	82	86
Government-sponsored enterprise stock[7]	109	109	109	109	109	109	109	109	109	109	109	109
Air carrier worker support warrants and notes[8]	5	13	13	13	13	13	13	12	12	12	12	7
Non-Federal securities held by NRRIT	24	24	22	20	18	17	15	13	11	10	9	8
Other assets net of liabilities	-73	-73	-73	-73	-73	-73	-73	-73	-73	-73	-73	-73
Total, financial assets net of liabilities	2,993	2,483	2,744	2,791	2,812	2,819	2,824	2,829	2,830	2,830	2,837	2,843
Debt held by the public net of financial assets	18,024	21,684	23,520	24,892	26,250	27,720	29,134	30,437	31,860	33,167	34,643	36,216
As a percent of GDP	85.8%	98.4%	100.1%	101.3%	102.8%	104.5%	105.8%	106.5%	107.3%	107.5%	107.9%	108.5%

* $500 million or less.

[1] A decrease in the Treasury operating cash balance (which is an asset) is a means of financing a deficit and therefore has a negative sign. An increase in checks outstanding (which is a liability) is also a means of financing a deficit and therefore also has a negative sign. More information on the levels and changes to the operating cash balance is available in Chapter 4, "Federal Borrowing and Debt," in the *Analytical Perspectives* volume of the Budget.

[2] Includes checks outstanding, accrued interest payable on Treasury debt, uninvested deposit fund balances, allocations of special drawing rights, and other liability accounts; and, as an offset, cash and monetary assets (other than the Treasury operating cash balance), other asset accounts, and profit on sale of gold.

[3] Consists mainly of debt issued by the Federal Financing Bank (which is not subject to limit), the unamortized discount (less premium) on public issues of Treasury notes and bonds (other than zero-coupon bonds), and the unrealized discount on Government account series securities.

[4] Legislation enacted August 2, 2019 (P.L. 116-37), temporarily suspends the debt limit through July 31, 2021.

[5] Treasury securities held by the public and zero-coupon bonds held by Government accounts are almost all measured at sales price plus amortized discount or less amortized premium. Agency debt securities are almost all measured at face value. Treasury securities in the Government account series are otherwise measured at face value less unrealized discount (if any).

[6] At the end of 2020, the Federal Reserve Banks held $4,445.5 billion of Federal securities and the rest of the public held $16,571.2 billion. Debt held by the Federal Reserve Banks is not estimated for future years.

[7] Treasury's warrants to purchase 79.9 percent of the common stock of the enterprises expire after September 7, 2028. The warrants were valued at $13 billion at the end of 2020.

[8] Of the notes and warrants issued under Air carrier worker support (Payroll support program), $0.5 billion are scheduled to expire by the end of 2026, $0.6 billion are scheduled to expire by the end of 2027, and $5.3 billion are scheduled to expire by the end of 2031.

OMB CONTRIBUTORS TO THE 2022 BUDGET

The following personnel contributed to the preparation of this publication. Hundreds, perhaps thousands, of others throughout the Government also deserve credit for their valuable contributions.

A

Lindsay Abate
Andrew Abrams
Chandana L. Achanta
Laurie Adams
Shagufta Ahmed
P. Joseph Ahn
Benjamin Aidoo
Lina Al Sudani
Joseph Albanese
Isabel Aldunate
Jason Alleman
Victoria Allred
Aaron Alton
Michaela Amos
Kimberly Anoweck
Nickole M. Arbuckle
Rachel Arguello
Alison Arnold
Aviva Aron-Dine
Anna R. Arroyo
Emily Schultz Askew
Lisa L. August

B

Samuel Bagenstos
Drew Bailey
Jessie W. Bailey
Ally P. Bain
Paul W. Baker
Steven Bakovic
Carol A. Bales
Caroline Ball
Pratik S. Banjade
Avital Bar-Shalom
Zachary Barger
Carl Barrick
Jody Barringer
Alexander Barron
Amy Batchelor
Sarah Belford
Jennifer Wagner Bell
Sara Bencic

Joseph J. Berger
Danielle Berman
Elizabeth A. Bernhard
Katherine Berrey
William Bestani
Samuel J. Black
Sharon Block
Kate Bloniarz
Mathew C. Blum
Tia Boatman
   Patterson
Sharon A. Boivin
Amira C. Boland
Cassie L. Boles
Melissa B. Bomberger
Derick A. Boyd Jr.
William J. Boyd
Michael Branson
Alex M. Brant
Joseph F. Breighner
Andrea M. Brian
Candice M. Bronack
Ashley A. Brooks
Katherine W. Broomell
Dustin S. Brown
Sheila Bruce
Michael T. Brunetto
Nicole Budzinski
Pearl Buenvenida
Tom D. Bullers
Scott H. Burgess
Ben Burnett
Jordan C. Burris
John C. Burton
Nicholas S. Burton
Mark Bussow
Dylan W. Byrd

C

Steven Cahill
Greg Callanan
Amy Canfield
Eric D. Cardoza

Kevin Carpenter
Curtis M. Carr Jr.
Christina S. Carrere
Matthew Carroll
William S. S. Carroll
Scott D. Carson
Corryne C. Carter
Mary I. Cassell
David Cerrato
Dan Chandler
Anthony Chase
James Chase
Nida Chaudhary
Erin Cheese
Anita Chellaraj
Damon Clark
Michael Clark
Sean Coari
Alyssa Cogen
Jordan Cohen
Pamela Coleman
Victoria W. Collin
Debra M. Collins
Kelly T. Colyar
Jose A. Conde
Alyson M. Conley
David C. Connolly
Kyle Connors
Mary Rose Conroy
Shila Cooch
LaTiesha B. Cooper
Benjamin E. Coyle
Drew W. Cramer
Ayana Crawford
William Creedon
Jill L. Crissman
Rose Crow
Jefferson Crowder
James Crowe
Juliana Crump
Craig Crutchfield
David M. Cruz-
   Glaudemans
Lily Cuk

Pennee Cumberlander
C. Tyler Curtis
William Curtis
Matthew Cutts

D

J. Alex Dalessio
D. Michael Daly
Rody Damis
Neil B. Danberg
Elisabeth C. Daniel
Kristy L. Daphnis
Alexander J. Daumit
Joanne C. Davenport
Kelly Jo Davis
Kenneth L. Davis
Margaret B. Davis-
   Christian
Karen De Los Santos
Tasha M. Demps
Paul J. Denaro
Kimberly A. Denz
Catherine A. Derbes
Christopher DeRusha
Suzy Deuster
John H. Dick
Jamie Dickinson
Amie Didlo
Rachel M. Diedrick
Jean Diomi Kazadi
Angela M. Donatelli
Paul S. Donohue
Cristin Dorgelo
Vladik Dorjets
Michelle Dorsey
Celeste Drake
Megan Dreher
Lisa Cash Driskill
Mark A. Dronfield
Abigail Drucis
Vanessa Duguay
Nathaniel Durden
Ryan Durga

Reena Duseja

E

Matthew C. Eanes
Jacqueline A. Easley
Calie Edmonds
Jeanette Edwards
Matthew Eliseo
Michelle Enger
Diana F. Epstein
Brede Eschliman
Robert Etter
Beatrix Evans
Gillian Evans
Patrick Evans

F

Farnoosh Faezi-Marian
Robert Fairweather
Edna Falk Curtin
Hunter Fang
Christine E.
  Farquharson
Louis Feagans
Iris R. Feldman
Christopher M. Felix
Kelsi Feltz
Lesley A. Field
Sean C. Finnegan
Mary Fischietto
John J. Fitzpatrick
Cleones Fleurima
Daniel G. Fowlkes
Nicholas A. Fraser
Rob Friedlander
Laurel Fuller
Steven Furnagiev

G

Abigail P. Gage
Scott D. Gaines
Christopher D.
  Gamache
Joseph R. Ganahl
Kyle Gardiner
Mathias A. Gardner
Arpit Garg
Marc Garufi
Anthony R. Garza
Anna M. Gendron
Mariam Ghavalyan

Daniel Giamo
Carolyn Gibson
Brian Gillis
Jacob Glass
Joshua S. Glazer
Porter O. Glock
Andrea L. Goel
Jeffrey D. Goldstein
Christopher Gomba
Anthony A. Gonzalez
Oscar Gonzalez
Alex Goodenough
Michael D. Graham
David M. Gratz
Aron Greenberg
Brandon H. Greene
Robin J. Griffin
Justin Grimes
Hester C. Grippando
Stephanie F. Grosser
Andrea L. Grossman
Kerry Gutknecht

H

Michael B. Hagan
James R. Hagen
Jessica K. Hale
Tia Hall
Victor Hall
William F. Hamele
Christine E. Hammer
Brian Hanson
Jennifer L. Hanson
Dionne Hardy
Deidre A. Harrison
Edward Hartwig
Paul Harvey
Abdullah Hasan
Laurel Havas
Nichole M. Hayden
Mark Hazelgren
Kelly Healton
Gary Hellman
John David Henson
Matthew A. Herb
Rachel Hernández
Alex Hettinger
Michael J. Hickey
Michael Hildner
Amanda M. Hill
Jonathan Hill
Walter F. Hill
Michelle Hilton

Elke Hodson-Marten
Jennifer E. Hoef
Stuart Hoffman
Troy Holland
Brian Holm-Hansen
Javay C. Holmes
Michele Holt
Jack Hoskins
Clinton T. Hourigan
Aaron B. House
Peter Hoy
Grace Hu
Rhea A. Hubbard
Kathy M. Hudgins
Shristi Humagai
Ashley Hungerford
Sally J. Hunnicutt
Alexander T. Hunt
Lorraine D. Hunt
James C. Hurban
Veta Hurst

I

Tae H. Im

J

Scott W. Jackson
Manish Jain
Harrison M. Jarrett
Ames R. Jenkins
Carol Jenkins
Connor Jennings
Julie Jent
Carol Johnson
Michael D. Johnson
Danielle Y. Jones
Denise Bray Jones
Lauren H. Jones
Lisa M. Jones
Shannon Maire Joyce
Hursandbek
  Jumanyazov
Hee Jun

K

Kosta Kalpos
Daniel S. Kaneshiro
Jacob H. Kaplan
Jenifer L. Karwoski
Regina L. Kearney
Benjamin R. Keffer

Christopher Keller
Mary W. Keller
Nancy B. Kenly
Moses I. Kennedy
Jung H. Kim
Maria Kim
Michael B. Kim
Rachael Y. Kim
Kelly C. King
Kelly A. Kinneen
Marina Kirakosian
Jessica Elizabeth
  Kirby
Robert T. Klein
Ellen Knight
Bobby Kogan
Nick Koo
Andrea G. Korovesis
Katelyn V. Koschewa
A. Faride Kraft
Charles Kraiger
Lori A. Krauss
Megan K. Kruse
Steven B. Kuennen
Jennifer J. Kuk
Christine J. Kymn

L

Christopher D. LaBaw
Sherry Lachman
Leonard L. Lainhart
Chad A. Lallemand
Lawrence L. Lambert
Michael Landry
Daniel LaPlaca
Eric P. Lauer
Jessie L. LaVine
Daniel Lawver
Jessica Lee
Susan E. Leetmaa
Carmine Leggett
Bryan P. León
Kerrie Leslie
Ariel Leuthard
John Levock-Spindle
Sheila Lewis
Andrew Lieberman
Jennifer Liebschutz
Jane C. Lien
Kristina E. Lilac
Erika Liliedahl
Michael Linden
John E. Lindner

Jennifer M. Lipiew
Adam Lipton
Kim Lopez
Sara R. Lopez
Adrienne Lucas

M

Ryan MacMaster
Christian MacMillan
Claire A. Mahoney
Mayur Manchanda
Dominic J. Mancini
Caroline Manela
Noah S. Mann
Iulia Z. Manolache
Roman Manziyenko
Chris Marokov
Italy Martin
Rochelle Martinez
Nicole Martinez Moore
Clare Martorana
Kimie Matsuo
Joshua May
Steven McAndrews
Jessica Rae McBean
Alexander J.
   McClelland
John L. McClung
Malcolm P. McConnell
Jeremy P. McCrary
Anthony W. McDonald
Christine A. McDonald
Katrina A. McDonald
Renford McDonald
Michael McManus
William McNavage
Christopher McNeal
Andrea Medina-Smith
Edward Meier
Barbara A. Menard
Flavio Menasce
Margaret Mergen
P. Thaddeus
   Messenger
William L. Metzger
Lauren Michaels
Daniel J. Michelson-
   Horowitz
Eric Mill
Jason Miller
Kimberly Miller
Sofie Miller
Susan M. Minson

Emily A. Mok
Kirsten J. Moncada
Claire Monteiro
Joseph Montoni
Andrea J. Montoya
Julia C. Moore
Betty T. Morrison
Josephine Morse
Savannah M. Moss
Austin B. Mudd
Robin McLaughry
   Mullins
Daenuka
   Muraleetharan
Jonathan J. Murphy
Christian G. Music
Hayley W. Myers
Kimberley L Myers

N

Jeptha E. Nafziger
Larry J. Nagl
Barry Napear
Robert Nassif
Kimberly P. Nelson
Michael D. Nelson
Anthony Nerino
Melissa K. Neuman
Joanie F. Newhart
Kimberly Armstrong
   Newman
Christine Nguy
Tim H. Nusraty
Joseph B. Nye

O

Erin O'Brien
Kerry Clinton O'Dell
Melanie Ofiesh
Matthew J. O'Kane
Kathryn Olson
Brendan J. O'Meara
Matthew Oreska
Lydia H. Orth
Jared Ostermiller

P

Heather C. Pajak
Farrah N. Pappa
Jacob A. Parcell
John C. Pasquantino

Michael Pauls
Brian Paxton
Casey Pearce
Michael D. Pearlstein
Liuyi Pei
Falisa L. Peoples-Tittle
Emma C. Perron
Michael A. Perz
Whitney L. Peters
William C. Petersen
Andrea M. Petro
Amy E. Petz
Stacey Que-Chi Pham
Alec Pharris
Carolyn R. Phelps
Karen A. Pica
Brian Pickeral
Brian Pipa
Joseph Pipan
Maggie Polachek
Mark J. Pomponio
Ruxandra Pond
Julianne Poston
Larrimer S. Prestosa
Jamie M. Price
Alanna B. Pugliese
Robert B. Purdy

R

Lucas R. Radzinschi
K. Sabeel Rahman
Houman Rasouli
Johnnie Ray
Alex Reed
Thomas M. Reilly
Bryant D. Renaud
Keri A. Rice
Natalie Rico
Kyle S. Riggs
Jamal Rittenberry
Maria Roat
Beth Higa Roberts
Donovan Robinson
Marshall J. Rodgers
Jung M. Roh
Samantha Romero
Meredith B. Romley
Renee Rosa
Jeffrey R. Ross
David J. Rowe
Amanda Roy
Danielle Royal
Brian Rozental

Tamia Russell
Erika H. Ryan

S

Adam N. Salazar
John Asa Saldivar
Mark S. Sandy
Nathan T. Sanfilippo
Ruth Saunders
Gregoire F. Sauter
Joel Savary
Jason K. Sawyer
Rio Schondelmeyer
Daniel K. Schory
Mariarosaria
   Sciannameo
Kristi Scott
Jasmeet K. Seehra
Kimberly Segura
Robert B. Seidner
Andrew Self
Megan Shade
Shabnam
   Sharbatoghlie
Amy K. Sharp
Dianne Shaughnessy
Paul Shawcross
Andrew B. Shea
Gary F. Shortencarrier
Matthew Sidler
Leticia Sierra
Sara R. Sills
Angela Simmons
Celeste Simon
Daniel Liam Singer
Sarah Sisaye
Robert Sivinski
Benjamin J. Skidmore
Evan C. Skloot
Curtina O. Smith
Sarah B. Smith
Stannis M. Smith
Silvana Solano
Roderic A. Solomon
Timothy F. Soltis
Amanda R.K. Sousane
Candice G. Spalding
Rebecca L. Spavins
Valeria Spinner
Christopher Spiro
John H. Spittell
Sarah Whittle Spooner
Travis C. Stalcup

Scott R. Stambaugh
Nora Stein
Ryan Stoffers
Gary R. Stofko
Terry W. Stratton
Vanessa D. Studer
Thomas J. Suarez
Kevin J. Sullivan
Patrick Sullivan
Jessica L. Sun
Ariana Sutton-Grier
Katherine M. Sydor

T

Jamie R. Taber
Naomi S. Taransky
Myra L. Taylor
Jay F. Teitelbaum
Emma K. Tessier
Amanda L. Thomas
Barbara E. Thomas
Judith F. Thomas
Payton A. Thomas
Will Thomas

Serita K. Thornton
Parth Tikiwala
Thomas Tobasko
Gia Tonic
Gil M. Tran
Vy Tran
Susanna Troxler
Austin Turner

U

Nicholas J. Ufier
Shraddha A.
   Upadhyaya
Darrell J. Upshaw
Taylor J. Urbanski

V

Matthew J. Vaeth
Candace Vahlsing
Areletha L. Venson
Alexandra Ventura
Cesar Villanueva
Megha Vyas

W

James A. Wade
Brett Waite
Nicole Waldeck
Joseph Waldow
Traci Walker
Heather V. Walsh
Tim Wang
Ben Ward
Peter H. Waterman
Gary Waxman
Bess M. Weaver
Jacqueline K. Webb
Daniel Week
William J. Weinig
David Weisshaar
Lillian Welch
Philip R. Wenger
Max West
Arnette C. White
Ashley M. White
Curtis C. White
Kim S. White
Sherron R. White

Brian Widuch
Jeremy D. Williams
Alex O. Wilson
James Wolff
Minzy Won
Alegra Woodard
Sophia M. Wright
Bert Wyman

Y

Danny Yagan
Melany N. Yeung
David Y. Yi
Christian T. Yonkeu
Xia You
Frank Young
Rita Young
Shalanda D. Young
Janice Yun

Z

Eliana M. Zavala
Erica H. Zielewski

www.ingramcontent.com/pod-product-compliance
Lightning Source LLC
Chambersburg PA
CBHW081722270326
41933CB00017B/3255